SOUTH EAST

Nicholas King

Capital Transport

CONTENTS

ISBN 185414 150 3

Published by Capital Transport Publishing
38 Long Elmes, Harrow Weald, Middlesex

Printed by The KPC Group, Ashford, Kent

© Capital Transport Publishing 1992

The front cover photo is by C.D.Jones
The back cover photos are by Paul Gainsbury and Mike Harris
The frontispiece is by A.Gilmour

ALDER VALLEY

Alder Valley Ltd, Halimote Road, Aldershot, Hampshire, GU11 3EG

Alder Valley was renamed from Alder Valley South on 1st January 1989, having been formed on 1st January 1986 when the Thames Valley & Aldershot Omnibus Company Ltd was divided, and thus reverted in many respects to the former Aldershot & District operation.

The company was sold to Q Drive (Len Wright group) on 18th November 1988, having been purchased from the National Bus Company by Frontsource Ltd in October 1987. Its area covers north-east Hampshire and parts of south-west Surrey. Most Surrey operations were transferred to Randomquick Ltd in December 1990 and subsequently absorbed by London Country South West Ltd. In October 1992 the remaining part of Alder Valley was sold to the Stagecoach group though the LondonLink work went to The Bee Line's Bracknell depot.

The fleet is painted in light green livery with yellow relief and dark green skirt. A Dennis Loline from the former Aldershot & District fleet is retained in traditional livery. The fleet is allocated to garages at Aldershot, Alton and Hindhead.

Like most National Bus fleets, Alder Valley received large quantities of the standard Bristol VRT with Eastern Coach Works body to update their fleet and to enable pay-as-you-board conversion of crewed routes. No.615 was new in 1980 and is seen in Reading. Colin Lloyd

The number of Leyland Nationals operated by Alder Valley has declined in recent years, though some of the earliest remain in service. Those fitted with high-back seats were known as Suburban Express. Three of this type remain and 240 is seen in Buckingham Palace Road, London, while working service X8. Colin Lloyd

In 1992 Alder Valley received five Jonckheere Jubilee-bodied Volvos from sister company, The Bee Line. Used on the Londonlink service, 783 is seen near Victoria coach station, London. Colin Lloyd

Among the minibuses in the fleet are a dozen Iveco Daily vehicles with Robin Hood conversions. Many carry the Whippet insignia as shown by 478 in this view at Milford Station. Peter Relf

Alder Valley received ten Renault-Dodge S56 midibuses with Northern Counties bodywork during 1987 and 1988. The latter batch have raised bonnet arrangement, as seen by 418 photographed at Camberley station. Peter Relf

THE BEE LINE

The Berks Bucks Bus Co Ltd, Waterford House, Erftstadt Ct, Wokingham, Bucks, RG11 2XJ

The Berks Bucks Bus Co was established from 25th January 1987 as a renaming of Alder Valley North. This had been formed on 1st January 1986 following the division of the former Thames Valley & Aldershot Omnibus Company Ltd, and was sold by the NBC to Q Drive, part of the Len Wright group, in December 1987. The trading name 'The Bee Line' is used for local bus services together with a bee motif. The operational area closely corresponds with that of the former Thames Valley Traction Company.

During the autumn of 1986 a number of livery experiments took place resulting in the adoption of a livery of golden yellow with dark grey skirt for local buses, and variants have been developed for minibus operations.

Operations in the High Wycombe area were transferred to Oxford Bus Company in November 1990. The Londonlink service went to Reading Transport in October 1991 and the operations of Newbury and Reading followed in July 1992.

The fleet is operated from depots at Bracknell and Maidenhead.

Five Leyland Olympians were delivered in 1988 and featured Northern Counties bodywork. Based at Bracknell, they are usually to be found on the Reading service. Colin Lloyd

A substantial presence of VRs remains in the Bee Line fleet, though some were sold to Reading Transport in July 1992. No.527 is seen at the beginning of that month just prior to transfer.

The Bee Line fleet contains many Leyland Nationals purchased under National Bus control. New in 1976, No.382 is one of the batch of the Suburban Express model, fitted with high-back seating and higher gearing. Though this vehicle has recently been sold to Reading Buses, others remain in the fleet. Colin Lloyd

Following the arrival in 1987 of 22 Mercedes-Benz 609D minibuses with Robin Hood bodywork, a batch of 10 Optare StarRider bodied Mercedes arrived in 1988-89. The addition of offside legal lettering, a feature of The Bee Line, can be seen in this picture of 205. Colin Lloyd

The Bee Line Rail-Air link has featured many types of coach designs over the years. The latest examples are seven Berkhof Excellence 2000, built on the Scania K113CRB chassis. At Heathrow, preparing for departure, is 746. Malcolm King

BRIGHTON BUSES

Brighton Borough Transport Ltd, Coombe Terrace, Lewes Road, Brighton, BN2 4AQ

Brighton Borough Transport derives from the former Brighton Corporation operation which opened on 25th November 1901 with a network of 25 trams. Motor-buses were introduced on 1st April 1939, followed in May by trolleybuses. Trams were withdrawn on 31st August 1939 and trolleybuses last ran on 31st December 1960. For many years pooling arrangements were conducted with Brighton, Hove & District and also latterly with Southdown.

Deregulation in October 1986 was anticipated by the adoption of the present fleet title in March 1986, covering Brighton Buses, Brighton Coaches and, for non-operational activities, Brighton Transport. The 11-vehicle fleet of Chapman, Lewes, was purchased in May 1988 and the fleetname of Lewes Coaches retained for operations. On 30th June 1989 the Campings Luxury Coaches business was purchased and continues a separate division. Vehicles for the Lewes operation have gradually been integrated into the main fleet.

The fleet operates in a livery of light blue and white with dark blue skirt and lining and black window-surrounds. Vehicles are kept at the garage in Lewes Road, Brighton with outstations at Meadow Road, Worthing, and on Cliffe Industrial Estate, Lewes.

The oldest vehicles of the Brighton Buses fleet still in regular use are the eight Leyland Atlanteans of 1976/7 with East Lancashire bodywork. Belying its age, No.67 circumnavigates Palmeira Square, Hove in April 1992. E.C. Churchill

Representing the newer order is No.21, a Dennis Dominator with East Lancashire body delivered in 1985, one of a pair fitted with coach seating. Older Dominators acquired from Tayside have since been withdrawn. Andrew Gainsbury

Three Leyland Nationals with dual-purpose seating were acquired from Crosville Wales in 1990. No.78, carrying Lewes Coaches fleetnames, prepares to depart from Eastbourne Station on 2nd May 1992. Roy Marshall

Two ex-Southend Leyland Leopards had their coach bodywork replaced by new Willowbrook bus examples in 1991, being re-registered in the process. No.81 waits in Crawley Bus Station in August 1992 on a Lewes Coaches working. Mike Harris

New single-deckers in 1990 were five Leyland Lynxes, joining earlier examples of the type. No.95 passes through Brighton town centre in April 1991. Colin Lloyd

Still going strong are three of the 1968 Leyland Titans with MCW/Cammell Laird bodywork converted to open-top. No.32 shows the special livery used for the Countrybus open-top service in this view. Malcolm King

The Brighton minibus fleet now comprises 15 Renault-Dodge vehicles with Alexander conversions. No.60 was seen in Crawley Bus Station working for Lewes Coaches on 10th April 1991. Colin Lloyd

BRIGHTON & HOVE

Brighton & Hove Bus and Coach Co. Ltd, Conway Street, Hove, East Sussex, BN3 3LT

The present fleetname was adopted from 21st April 1986 following the transfer of the Brighton & Hove activities from Southdown into a separate division on 1st March 1985. The former Brighton, Hove & District Ltd company had been reactivated from 1st January 1986 for this purpose. The firm was sold by the National Bus Company to a management-led team in May 1987.

From the autumn of 1985 the fleet was gradually repainted into a distinctive new livery of cream with black skirt and dark red bands on the lower panels flying to the roof at the rear axle. The fleet was also renumbered from the former Southdown system into a three-digit scheme. An elderly Bristol KSW6G was retrieved from private ownership in 1986 and carries traditional livery.

The fleet is housed in garages at Hove and Whitehawk and at outstations in Newhaven, Shoreham and Steyning.

Amongst the many Bristol VRTs in the Brighton & Hove fleet are nine with dual-door convertible open-top bodywork by Eastern Coach Works. No.603 was working in covered-top form on 25th April 1992, with another of the batch in close pursuit. G.R. Mills

Thirty Scanias with East Lancashire bodywork joined the fleet from 1988 to 1990. No.714 passes through Eastbourne on the coastal route to Brighton on 2nd May 1992. Roy Marshall

Most Leyland Nationals in the fleet are of the Mk2 type. No.155 was one of the final batch delivered to Southdown in 1985 and came into the Brighton & Hove fleet when that was set up in 1986. It is seen in the centre of Brighton on 11th March 1992. Terry Blackman

Nine Dennis Javelins were purchased from 1988 to 1990. No.507, with Duple 320 coachwork, was the first of the 1990 batch. Malcolm King

When Bournemouth withdrew their Mercedes-Benz/Wadham Stringer minibus fleet in 1990 after only a few months' use, Brighton & Hove quickly acquired all but one. No.354 is seen in Brighton. Andrew Jarosz

Brighton & Hove operate two Peugeot-Talbot Pullman six-wheel vehicles on behalf of East Sussex County Council. No.420 demonstrates the lack of support for these routes in Whitehawk Way during June 1992. David Harman

EASTBOURNE BUSES

Eastbourne Buses Ltd, Birch Road, Eastbourne, East Sussex, BN23 6PD

Municipal bus operation started in Eastbourne in 1903 being a world first. As a result of deregulation legislation services are now marketed as Eastbourne Buses. From May 1987 Eastbourne collaborated with Southdown in the Hastings Top Line venture until selling out their share in September 1989.

The once-substantial presence of Leyland Atlanteans in the fleet has almost been eliminated, though secondhand vehicles of this type have joined the fleet. Dennis Dominators and Leyland Olympians now form the majority of double deckers, together with an increasing number of Dennis single-deckers, with Dennis Lance models currently on order. Various secondhand Leyland Nationals have also appeared.

Fleet colours are biscuit and aircraft blue for buses, while coaches bear biscuit with red and blue, or various tones of blue stripes. All vehicles are accommodated at the Birch Road headquarters.

The golden era is remembered by No.81, an unusual Leyland PD3/11 with Metro-Cammell bodywork new to Blackpool in 1968 and acquired in 1989, though rarely seen in service. Roy Marshall

The Dennis Dominator was the standard Eastbourne double decker in the early 1980s, East Lancs bodywork being fitted. No.44 is one of the last batch, delivered in 1982. Roy Marshall

The largest single batch of vehicles in the fleet comprises 12 Leyland Olympians with Northern Counties bodywork purchased in 1988. No.57 is seen on rail replacement work at Eastbourne Station in April 1992.
David Harman

Open-top operation is still a feature of the Eastbourne scene. No.65 is a Leyland Atlantean with Eastern Coach Works body, acquired from Ipswich in 1980 and converted to open-top in 1985. The name 'Eastbourne Queen' is carried on the lower front panel. This view was taken at Beachy Head in May 1991.
Terry Blackman

Similar vehicle No.66 shows the different colours applied in its role as 'Eastbourne King' at a service for the RH&DR rally at New Romney Station on 21st June 1992.
David Harman

The Dennis Dart has found favour with Eastbourne. No.9 was new in 1990 with a Wadham Stringer 'Portsdown' body and was found loading at Eastbourne Station in this view. Malcolm King

More recent arrivals have included Dennis Javelins for bus work. No.24 has Wadham Stringer 'Vanguard' bodywork, seen at Hastings Station on 29th March 1992. Paul Gainsbury

Eastbourne Buses No.10, a Dennis Javelin with Duple 300 55-seat bus body, was new in 1990. This view at Cornfield Road, Eastbourne demonstrates how Eastbourne have expanded into the rural East Sussex area since deregulation. Andrew Gainsbury

Recent years have seen an influx of Leyland Nationals to the Eastbourne fleet, some lasting longer than others. No.12 was acquired from London Country North West in 1990 and was seen in Bexhill during April 1992 on an ESCC Thursday-only tendered service. Terry Blackman

EAST KENT

East Kent Road Car Co Ltd, North Lane, Canterbury, Kent, CT2 7DX

East Kent was formed in 1916 by the amalgamation of five local operators. Alone among the larger public operators in this volume it has retained both its independent identity and operating area during the upheavals of the past 20 years, although sharing common management with Maidstone & District for some six years up to 1983. The operating area is broadly defined as east of a line drawn from Faversham through Ashford across the Romney Marsh to Lydd, but with services extending to Maidstone and Hastings. East Kent was sold by the NBC to a management-led team on 5th March 1987. In November 1987 the firm of Marinair Coach Services, Cliftonville was purchased and absorbed within the main fleet.

As well as its network of local bus operations, East Kent retains an involvement in National Express and other contract work for tour operators, superstores and the Canterbury Park & Ride scheme. Excursions, extended holiday and private hire coaching work are also undertaken. There is also a significant commitment to courtesy services at Dover for cross-Channel carriers, but the once extensive involvement in staff transport to the four collieries in the East Kent coalfield ended with the closure of the last in August 1989.

Buses and coaches are painted in a livery of burgundy and cream with a stylised fleet logo. Minibuses operate in yellow with red and black relief as EK Minilink. Vehicles operate from garages at Ashford, Dover, Folkestone, Herne Bay and Westwood (Thanet) with outstations at Canterbury, New Romney and Deal.

East Kent responded to the need for intensive school peak traffic by purchasing ten Leyland Olympians with lengthened 85-seat Northern Counties bodywork in 1990. No.7802 demonstrates the breed at Folkestone Bus Station on 16th April 1991; note the 75th anniversary logo. Five of the type based at Herne Bay carry names with historic local connotations. Terry Blackman

To mark the 75th anniversary of operations in 1991, MCW Metrobus 2 No.7755 was repainted into traditional livery. Here it is seen leaving Folkestone Bus Station. *Malcolm King*

East Kent took large quantities of Bristol VRT/ECW vehicles to lowheight design to complete their one-man conversion plans. No.7666 is a 1980 example. *Malcolm King*

Amongst the declining number of Leyland Nationals in the fleet are eight with dual-purpose seating. No.1081, at Vicarage Lane, Ashford, is however working a local service normally the province of minibuses and is seen in the company of one of the operator's Iveco minibuses.
Malcolm King

The contract for a new Park-and-Ride scheme at Canterbury from the end of September 1991 led to the arrival of three Optare Deltas in a smart grey and dark blue livery. No.1401 takes layover at Gravel Walk, Canterbury.
Malcolm King

After initial batches of Ford Transits and Freight Rover Sherpas, the minibus fleet has standardised on the Iveco Daily. No.83, seen at Folkestone Bus Station, is one of the first batch bodied as 19-seaters by Robin Hood in 1987.
Ivor Norman

23

The famous West Gate at Canterbury proves a tight squeeze for modern double-deckers, especially those to full height configuration such as No.7986, a Bristol VRT with Willowbrook bodywork. John Grubb

The Sherpas in the fleet, converted locally by Dormobile, have been much reduced in number. A new route linking the Romney Marsh with Ashford to promote job access in 1991 has however provided a reprieve for No.36, which was found at Lydd-on-Sea with appropriate logos.

An unusual Leyland National in the fleet is No.1255, acquired in 1988 for dockside work at Dover. New in 1981 as an early example of the Mk2 type, it was initially used for development work by Dunlop at Coventry. This view shows it at Dover Priory Station in April 1991. Terry Blackman

MCW Metroliners represent a large proportion of the coaching fleet. The first batch arrived in 1983, displaying the rather flat-fronted appearance which was softened on later examples. No.8844 later received a registration from an open-top Regent, as seen here. Colin Lloyd

GREY-GREEN

T Cowie, 53-55 Stamford Hill, London N16 5TD

A new depot for Medway operations was opened in Strood in September 1988. Largely servicing commuter coach services to and from London, currently requiring fourteen vehicles, this has also been used as a foothold for Kent County Council contracts in the Tonbridge area, for which three Leyland Lynxes were acquired from Merthyr Tydfil at the end of 1989. Further morning and evening Kent County Council contracts were gained in the Medway Towns area during 1990-91 fiscal year.

From 29th March 1992, Grey-Green has taken over the operations of Allways, Sittingbourne, importing five Leyland Nationals from County Bus for further routes based in the Medway Towns.

Apart from six coaches in Eurolines livery, vehicles are painted in a coach livery of white with orange and green stripes or a bus livery of grey and green with orange and white relief.

At the end of March 1992 Grey-Green's Strood depot took over the local bus operations of Allen, Sittingbourne, acquiring five Leyland Nationals from County for the purpose. No.808 was found at Twydall Shops on the outskirts of Gillingham in May 1992. David Harman

Grey-Green were one of those to mop up Leyland Lynxes when the Merthyr Tydfil fleet collapsed in 1989. Three such vehicles are used for KCC routes in the Tonbridge area, such as No.802 in November 1990. Terry Blackman

THE KINGS FERRY

P S O'Neill, The Coach Station, Pump Lane, Gillingham, Kent

The Kings Ferry has a substantial presence in south east England, most notably on commuter services from the Medway Towns to London. Using high-specification coaches, these routes compare most favourably with the parallel Network SouthEast service although there is competition on the A2/M2 corridor with Grey Green and London Coaches.

From the early 1970s, when only half a dozen coaches were operated, Bedfords were purchased new while the fleet grew slowly. Heavyweight vehicles, Volvo and DAF arrived second-hand at the turn of the decade. From 1984, however, the fleet expanded rapidly to over 30 vehicles and the business was an early customer of Berkhof coachwork, initially on Volvo chassis.

By the end of the 1980s, with a fleet of over 50 vehicles, expansion had peaked and numbers have remained steady while fleet renewal has taken place.

The Kings Ferry have maintained a modern image for commuter services and associated private hire work. No.5.5 combines a Volvo B10M-60 chassis and Caetano Algarve coachwork, and was new in 1989.
Colin Lloyd

The KFC registration mark has been appropriated in substantial numbers for deliveries in 1991 and 1992. No.4.4, a Mercedes-Benz 0303/2, arrives at Buckingham Palace Road on 20th September 1991.
Colin Lloyd

MAIDSTONE & DISTRICT

The Maidstone & District Motor Services Ltd, Luton Road, Chatham, Kent, ME5 7LH

Maidstone & District was formed in 1911 and at one time held sway throughout the western half of Kent and into East Sussex. Today its operations are rather more compact, taking in the Medway Towns, Maidstone, Tonbridge, Tunbridge Wells and the Swale area, together with a presence in the Weald area. There is a strong London service from the Medway Towns and Maidstone, marketed under the 'Invictaway' banner.

Maidstone & District was one of the first National Bus subsidiaries to be privatised when it was sold to a management team on 6th November 1986, through Einkorn Ltd, an off-the-shelf company. In June 1988 the competing New Enterprise Coaches of Tonbridge was bought out. This operation continues as a subsidiary within the Einkorn group. On 12th June the residual vehicles of Boro'line Maidstone were purchased, together with the Maidstone depot.

The new management has shown much enterprise in handling the development of the company. Minibuses have made their inexorable appearance in all the major traffic centres, and vehicle purchasing policy has included Leyland Olympians, together with secondhand Dennis Dominators and Leyland Atlanteans.

Fleet livery is grass green with cream relief. Coaches and Invictaway vehicles carry NBC-based schemes using these colours. The fleet operates from garages at Edenbridge, Hawkhurst, Medway Towns (Luton and Gillingham), Maidstone and Tunbridge Wells, with outstation locations at Sheerness, Sittingbourne and Tenterden. The New Enterprise fleet has its own site in Tonbridge.

Twenty Fleetlines were purchased from London Transport in 1982 and converted to single-door format. No.5026 has Park Royal bodywork on Leyland-built chassis and was found at Chatham.
Richard Lewis

Six Dennis Dominators purchased for NBC evaluation trials in 1980 have been followed by 13 secondhand examples of the type. No.5315 carries East Lancashire bodywork and came from the East Staffordshire fleet in 1985. Here it is seen in New Cut, Chatham.
John Grubb

Further reinforcements to the double-deck fleet arrived in 1987/8 in the shape of 15 Leyland Atlanteans with Northern Counties bodies surplus to the requirements of Greater Manchester. All now operate at Maidstone. No.5724 departs from the Chequers Centre bus mall at Maidstone on 8th October 1991.
Terry Blackman

By far the main double-deck type is still the Bristol VRT with Eastern Coach Works body. No.5854 was found in Gravesend, now a mere outpost of the operating area, on 18th January 1992. The depot at Borough Green from which it was working was closed in August 1992. Colin Lloyd

All of the Metrobus 2s are allocated to Luton (Chatham) depot. No.5201, the first of the batch, awaits departure in Gravesend on 18th January 1992. The livery continues to use the NBC shade of grass green. Richard Eversden

The first NBC evaluatory Dennis Dominator with Alexander bodywork moved to M&D as their No.5300 after trials with Potteries, and was to presage several such acquisitions in the fleet. Malcolm King

Only one batch of Dominators has however been purchased new by M&D, comprising six vehicles with Willowbrook bodywork in 1980. No.5302 approaches the Chatham Pentagon Bus Station in this view. Malcolm King

The same location shows one of the 1990 batch of Leyland Olympians with Northern Counties bodywork. The roof fleet numbers, formerly used to assist vehicle identification in Chatham Bus Station, are now being discontinued. *Malcolm King*

Service expansion in Maidstone from December 1991 has led to the acquisition of seven Leyland Atlanteans from Luton & District. No.5737, with Roe bodywork, was the first to receive full M&D livery and was photographed at Gillingham Bus Station. *Malcolm King*

KCC requirements have led to the arrival of six Dennis Darts with Plaxton bodywork to DiPTAC specification. Three are used at Tenterden on routes to Ashford and Tunbridge Wells. No.3466 loads at Monson Road, Tunbridge Wells in its first days in service during June 1992. David Harman

M&D still have seven of their coach-seated Leyland Olympians with Eastern Coach Works bodies, though a decline in traffic on Invictaway routes has led to two of these being repainted in this striking livery for use on the long route 5 from Maidstone to Hastings. No.5442 pulls past Robertsbridge Station on April 1992 on a diversion occasioned by roadworks. Paul Gainsbury

Maidstone Park-and-Ride services involve four Mercedes-Benz 25-seaters, of which the most recent, No.1204, has Carlyle bodywork. Here it is found at the Willington Street terminal of the original Park-and-Ride service.
Richard Lewis

Coaching operation has been slimmed to the bare bones in recent years, and is mainly resourced by four modern Leyland Tigers based at Gillingham. No.C189 has Duple 340 coachwork and was new in 1989. Colin Lloyd

OXFORD

City of Oxford Motor Services Ltd, Cowley Road, Oxford, OX4 2DJ

The Oxford Bus Company, as it is now marketed, was sold by the NBC to a management-led team on 15th January 1987. Operations are largely confined to Oxford and the surrounding area, other routes having been transferred to the offshoot South Midland company which in turn was taken over by Thames Transit in December 1988. However, the High Wycombe operations of Berks Bucks were absorbed in November 1990 and are operated as a separate unit. Wycombe Bus has the first Leyland Nationals to be owned by City of Oxford. There is a frequent City Link service along the M40, to London, together with a similar service direct to Heathrow and Gatwick airports. Another interesting operation is the Park-and-Ride service between outlying car parks and the city centre.

A livery is used of dark red with white roof and black skirt though some vehicles still carry the former livery of poppy red with white relief. City Link vehicles carry a livery of dark blue, deep yellow and white, applied in NBC style.

The fleet is garaged at the main address and at High Wycombe.

Oxford 999, a prototype for the Leyland Olympian, performed demonstration work for Leyland in the Far East with its Alexander body. Since returning in 1987 it has worked the Park & Ride service and is seen at one of the car park termini. Malcolm King

Many of the 1976 Alder Valley delivery of Bristol VRTs found their way to High Wycombe depot, and hence passed to Oxford with that operation in 1990. While still operated as a separate entity to the Oxford base, most of the fleet have been repainted into Oxford's colours, now seen in many parts of Berkshire. Reading is the setting for 1543, heading for home. Colin Lloyd

Oxford were early purchasers of the Eastern Coach Works-bodied Leyland Olympian. Typical of the type is 224, seen in Oxford city centre. Terry Blackman

Five production examples of Alexander's RL design arrived in 1988 and two years later a further six similarly bodied Olympians joined the fleet. No.234 is one of the second batch and was photographed in July 1992. Colin Lloyd

Having eschewed the Leyland National for eighteen years, Oxford found themselves inheritors of the type with the acquisition of the High Wycombe operation of The Bee Line in 1990. Now in Wycombe livery is 1335, a 1975 example. Colin Lloyd

Six Leyland Leopard coaches have so far been re-bodied with Willowbrook Warrior bus bodies for further work. Crossing Cornmarket Street in plain white with black skirt is 611, still retaining its original registration mark. Peter Relf

Latest vehicles for the Oxford to London service are six Dennis Javelins fitted with the latest Plaxton Premiére bodywork. Photographed in London, shortly after delivery, is No.53. Colin Lloyd

PEOPLE'S PROVINCIAL

Provincial Bus Co Ltd, Gosport Road, Hoeford, Fareham, Hampshire, PO16 0ST

People's Provincial is the fleetname of the Provincial Bus Company which was the successor to the Provincial Tramways Company Ltd which started horse tramways in Portsmouth in 1873. A subsidiary company, Gosport Tramways Company, started in 1884, again using horses. The Portsmouth operation passed to Portsmouth Corporation Tramways Department, but the Gosport tramway continued and was electrified in 1905. Motor buses were introduced in 1910 and the tramway was eventually replaced by Chevrolet buses in 1929 when the title of the company was changed to Gosport & Fareham Omnibus Company. This was a subsidiary of the Provincial Tramways Group and the Provincial fleetname was introduced. The company later passed into the hands of two other financial groups before it became part of the National Bus Company in 1970. To this small NBC unit was added the Fareham depots and operations of Hants & Dorset in 1983.

With the sale by the government of the National Bus Company operators, Provincial became an employee co-ownership scheme, the only former NBC fleet to be sold in this way.

In 1988 Peoples Provincial extended its day time operations into Portsmouth and since then Hampshire County Council tendered services have been secured. Notable among these are services formerly worked by Blue Admiral to the north of Portsmouth.

The livery has always been green. Originally an emerald shade relieved by cream, this was altered to NBC green and white from 1970. After privatisation a version similar to the original scheme was reintroduced with the addition of red wheels and 'People's Provincial' fleetnames.

The depot used is on the site of the original tram depot at Hoeford.

Leyland Nationals are the mainstay of the Provincial fleet, accounting for three-quarters of the total. Short and long, dual door and single door, bus and dual-purpose types are included. No.406, a short dual door vehicle, came from London Buses in 1991 to work on services formerly worked by Portsmouth Transit. A. Jarosz

Provincial's ACE Cougar No.333 is unique in the fleet. It carries a Wadham Stringer 'Portsdown' body 10.5m long and seating 41. Power is provided by a Perkins Phaser rear mounted engine. It normally works alongside Leyland Nationals on Portsmouth area services. Malcolm King

Open-top double deckers have long been a feature of the fleet and the latest additions are two former Bournemouth Fleetlines which were built as convertible open toppers in 1976. BVBG

The Iveco 49.10 is Provincial's standard minibus chassis and this type now numbers 24. The 1989 batch was fitted with Phoenix bodywork as shown on No.134 at Hedge End. A. Gilmour

A more recent Iveco is No.144. Malcolm King

READING TRANSPORT

Reading Transport Ltd, Mill Lane, Reading, Berkshire, RG1 2RW

Reading Transport took over the operations of the Reading Borough Council Transport Department on 26th October 1986. It operated stage services within the borough boundaries and express services to London. Following the acquisition of The Bee Line's Reading and Newbury duties in July 1992 the area of operation has increased.

The fleet remained stable during the latter half of the 1980s, but rapid withdrawals of the Scania Metropolitans that once formed a major component, have taken place. These have been replaced by Leyland Olympians and by fifteen second-hand MCW Metrobus 2s released from London Buses by tendering losses. Twelve Leyland Titans in the fleet represent the only significant purchase of the type in the South East outside London. The single-deck fleet has been developed with the arrival of midibuses, and the coaching presence has been strengthened by the acquisition, in October 1991, of The Bee Line's London services, together with some coaches. Further vehicles came with The Bee Line operations in July 1992.

A new fleet livery of cream, burgundy and aquamarine is now being introduced to replace the traditional maroon and cream on white. Vehicles used on London services are being painted into three-tone blue. Vehicles are based at the Mill Lane and Forbury, Reading and at Newbury.

Much of the Reading fleet is made up of MCW Metrobuses. No.154 is a typical example dating from 1979, photographed in the town.
Andrew Jarosz

The Leyland Titan found greater favour with Reading than with most other operators. No.73 is a late model from 1983 carrying bodywork assembled at Workington. Fitted with dual-doorway, it is seen on local service in Reading. Malcolm King

When London Buses withdrew the Mark II Metrobuses from Harrow Buses, the type was dispersed widely. The largest group is that with Reading, and 457 is seen in the town. Malcolm King

One of 12 dual-purpose MkII Metrobuses in the Reading fleet, No.143 is seen in the current livery for the Goldline private hire operation and service to London. Malcolm King

Arguably the star of the 1991 Bus and Coach show, Reading 701 is the first example of the Optare Spectra design, based on the purpose built DAF DB250HS underframe. It has been followed by two further examples for Reading. No.701 has been given the registration formerly carried by the mayor's car. Malcolm King

Following purchase of the MetroRider design, Optare made several subtle changes before production commenced in Leeds. Still basically the same shape, though much different mechanically, Reading 610 is seen in the company of one of Reading's ten Optare Deltas, which marked the undertaking's first significant entry into full-sized single-deck operation. Colin Lloyd

1991 saw Reading take over the rival London service from The Bee Line, together with five integral Hestair-Duple 425s. A new blue livery has now been introduced for the service and this is seen on 86, an Eastern Coach Works-bodied Leyland Olympian, and 242, one of the coaches acquired from The Bee Line. Colin Lloyd

SOLENT BLUE LINE

Musterphantom Ltd, 169-170 High Street, Southampton, SO1 0BY

Musterphantom was set up by Southern Vectis in May 1987 to compete with Southampton Citybus on services 16 and 17 using sixteen secondhand Bristol VRT's that were garaged on an industrial estate and operating under the Solent Blue Line name. Southampton responded by introducing a fleet of AEC Routemasters. In October 1987 Solent Blue Line acquired the Southampton operations of Hampshire Bus from the Stagecoach group, plus a number of routes in the Bishops Waltham area when the Hants & Sussex undertaking was taken over.

The mainland fleet totalled more than one hundred at this time but subsequent reorganisation has reduced this. In January 1988 a franchise arrangement was concluded, with Marchwood Motorways of Totton. The franchise has also included the Southampton to Petersfield route since March 1992. Although Marchwood have a minibus in Solent Blue Line livery, they have vehicles in a separate livery for Totton Link which is not part of the Solent Blue Line network.

The fleet is a common one with Southern Vectis and is shown as such in the fleet list. Livery for Solent Blue Line vehicles is yellow with two shades of blue. Minibuses are in a separate blue, yellow and orange livery. Solent Blue Line's depots are situated at Southampton, Eastleigh, Bishops Waltham, Eastleigh and Fawley.

Highbridge Bristol VRs 149-165 were used in the competitive era on services 16-18 against Southampton's Routemasters and were crew operated. Since the departure of the Routemasters, the conductors have disappeared and the batch of vehicles now appear on other services also.
Malcolm King

The Leyland Olympian has been the standard type of double decker for new purchases over the last five years. No.708, with coach seating, was delivered in 1989. Malcolm King

Eastleigh depot received the Mercedes 811Ds delivered in 1990 in a revised livery for midibuses of mid-blue, yellow and orange. The Phoenix bodies on these vehicles seat 31 and they are used on Hampshire County Council tendered services. A. Gilmour

Leyland National 417 in the Solent Blue Line fleet originated with Hants & Dorset, arriving in 1987 from Hampshire Bus. Typical of the numerous Leyland Nationals delivered to National Bus companies, it is seen at Southampton in February 1992. D.M. Loxley

The Iveco Daily is to be seen in the fleets of several southern operators, many of the type being fitted with Robin Hood bodywork. Typical of these vehicles, used both by Solent Blue Line and by parent Southern Vectis, is 278 seen in Eastleigh wearing Solent Blue Line minibus livery. D.M. Loxley

SOUTHAMPTON CITYBUS

Southampton Citybus Ltd, 226 Portswood Road, Southampton, Hampshire, SO9 4XS

This company was formed in October 1986 as the successor to Southampton City Transport. The traditional operating area is bounded by the M27 to the north, Totton in the West and Hedge End in the east though the operation of tendered services for Hampshire County Council and several commercial routes take Southampton Citybus vehicles well beyond Southampton. A certain amount of competition has also been experienced from Solent Blue Line on services 16 and 17 in Southampton and a fleet of crew operated Routemasters was acquired for these routes, though these buses have now been sold. A company, set up jointly with Badgerline, to compete in the Portsmouth area ran under the Red Admiral name. With the demise of the Portsmouth City undertaking Southampton Citybus took over the fleet under the Portsmouth Citybus name in June 1988 Citybus having a 75% interest.

The Red Admiral fleet was owned by Pathfinder Ltd in which Southampton held a 95% share. This fleet was transferred to Portsmouth Citybus in August 1989, though it is now part of Transit Holdings.

Fleet livery is red with a black skirt, most coaches are in overall red livery.

Southampton's single-deck fleet has been expanded in the last three years and includes 11 Leyland Lynxes, all of which sport grey skirt panels, wheelarches and lower grille panels. No.108 is pictured in the city centre. G.R. Mills

AN68/1 Atlanteans with East Lancashire bodywork still comprise the predominant bus type in the Southampton fleet. No.189 is seen in May 1992 still, apart from a few small dents, in good shape for its age. Malcolm King

No.292 is one of eight Dennis Dominators delivered in 1988 with coach styled but bus seated East Lancs bodywork. It was photographed in February 1992. D.M. Loxley

Southampton, like a number of other operators, has been experimenting with the rebodying of older vehicles. A batch of five 1974 Atlantean chassis has been thoroughly overhauled and fitted with new 35-seat single-deck bodywork by East Lancs. Malcolm King

No.10 is one of two open-top buses used by Southampton Citybus. It is used on tours of the City and a tour of Southampton Docks. Both the open toppers carry Red Admiral livery. Malcolm King

When Southampton purchased an interest in Portsmouth Citybus in 1988 several vehicles were passed to the Southampton fleet including three Dennis Lancets with Wadham Stringer bodywork. Two have since been sold and the remaining vehicle is now numbered 300. G.R. Mills

A single Carlyle bodied Dart arrived in 1990. It is seen on the Hospital Lynx service between the hospital and the city centre. G.R. Mills

The only Wadham-Stringer bodied Dart in the fleet is 307, a former demonstrator. Its 8.5 metre chassis is fitted with a Portsdown style body. G.R. Mills

Reeve Burgess bodywork is featured on the Dennis Dart purchased in 1991. It has a 9-metre chassis and is seen on service 52, which was worked as a franchise for Solent Blue Line for a period. G.R. Mills

SOUTHERN VECTIS

Southern Vectis Omnibus Company Ltd, Nelson Road, Newport, Isle of Wight, PO30 1RD

Southern Vectis was formed in 1929 when the Southern Railway Company took over the business of Dodson Brothers Ltd, trading as 'Vectis'. Services expanded and many smaller operators, both of stage carriage and tours, were acquired over the years until a near monopoly of services was attained. The company was nationalised in 1948 and passed to the National Bus Company in 1969. In October 1986 it became the third of National Bus Company subsidiaries to be sold when it was purchased by the company's own management. Further expansion took place in 1987 when the West Wight fleet, comprising four coaches, was acquired.

Expansion of a different kind took place in September 1987 when Southern Vectis, in conjunction with Badgerline, set up 'Badger Vectis' to compete with Wilts & Dorset on the Bournemouth/Poole corridor, though this operation ceased in March 1988.

The fleet is a combined one with Solent Blue Line and is shown as one in the fleet list. A notable feature is the operation of veteran vehicles on the Isle of Wight in their original liveries. Current fleet livery is emerald green and greensand for buses with silver grey for coaches, while some of the newer coaches are in National Express livery, with minibuses either red or blue. For the 1992 season the open top fleet are receiving a lime green and purple livery.

Deliveries of Olympians since 1989 have coach seated Leyland bodywork and Cummins L10 engines. No.725 looks very smart in Southern Vectis's standard green and cream livery. Malcolm King

Southern Vectis 102 is now on its third index-mark and second fleet number. Originally numbered 702 with matching A702DDL it is the survivor of a pair of Leyland Olympian express coaches. The mark displayed in the photograph has now been fitted to Leyland Tiger coach 310, while 102 now carries A295FDL. Colin Lloyd

Convertible open-top Bristol VR 503 was re-registered recently from UFX855S, thus hiding its Hants & Dorset origin. For the 1992 season it was painted in this tasteless but eyecatching purple and green livery. It is seen at Ryde depot. A. Gilmour

The oldest batch of VRs in service with Southern Vectis includes No.660, seen taking on passengers at Lake. M.S. Curtis

The operation of veteran vehicles on normal service is a well known feature of Southern Vectis. This 1960 Bristol FS lost its original registration for a time, but this has now been restored.

No.864 is a converted Bristol RE which works between Shanklin Railway Station and the Esplanade as 'Shanklin's Pony'. In this view however it is seen at Ventnor Bus Station. M.S. Curtis

Supplementing the 1956 Lodekka on the Yarmouth-Alum Bay service is Bristol KSG 502. Now in its 53rd year, it carries a restrained cream livery with green trim. M.S. Curtis

STAGECOACH SOUTH

Stagecoach South Ltd, 112 Malling Street, Lewes, East Sussex, BN7 2RB

The Stagecoach South group comprises the former Southdown, Hastings Buses and Hampshire Bus fleets. From 4th April 1992 the group was restructured into three divisions, with its head office at Lewes.

Stagecoach South Ltd, trading as Hampshire Bus, has depots at Andover, Basingstoke and Winchester and outstations at Botley and Petersfield. South Coast Buses Ltd trades as Southdown Buses in the Eastbourne area and as Hastings Buses in the Hastings and Rye area. In addition to depots at Eastbourne and Hastings there is a country depot at Rye and outstations at Lewes, Seaford and Uckfield.

Sussex Coastline Buses Ltd has depots at Chichester, Havent and Worthing, with outstations or sub-depots at Bognor Regis, Henfield, Littlehampton, Midhurst, Selsey and Storrington.

An increasing proportion of the fleet carries corporate Stagecoach livery, though vestiges can be seen of the constituent liveries, particularly in the east of the area. Regular interchanges of vehicles take place between the fleets, significantly as a result of the current delivery of 80 Dennis Darts with Alexander Dash bodywork. The allocation to individual areas at July 1992 is shown at the end of the fleet list. In October 1992 Alder Valley became part of the Stagecoach group though still run as a separate unit at present.

Stagecoach influence is increasingly evident with the arrival of new Leyland Olympians and the Dennis Darts. Rapid inroads are now being made into the older Leyland Nationals and non-standard types, though two Bristol REs survive in the Hastings fleet. Coaching operations, once a major part of the old Southdown fleet, are now concentrated in small units.

An order for 80 Dennis Darts with Alexander 'Dash' bodywork was under delivery in the summer of 1992. No.521 is the first in the South Coast Buses fleet, and was sent to Eastbourne to cover a route with physical restrictions. Malcolm King

For a while the Southdown version of Stagecoach livery included additional stripes of yellow, orange and blue around the front upper deck panels, as shown on Convertible open-top VR 621. Malcolm King

Southdown marked their 75th anniversary by repainting Bristol VRT/Eastern Coach Works No.276 into immaculate traditional livery. It was still so liveried in this view at Old Steine, Brighton in June 1992, though now translated to the more mundane ownership of Coastline. David Harman

Twelve Volvo Citybuses with Northern Counties coach-seated bodies were purchased in 1989 for longer inter-urban services. Three have since moved elsewhere in the Stagecoach empire following the arrival of newer Olympians and the rest are due to follow. No.307 is one of six still held by Coastline. Calvin Churchill

Early arrivals of Leyland Olympians with Alexander bodywork went into the Hampshire Bus fleet. No.202, constructed to carry no fewer than 87 seated passengers, was photographed in Basingstoke Bus Station. Peter Relf

Southdown's enforced withdrawal from Portsmouth in January 1991 led to six of the native Leyland National 2s being transferred across to Hastings, where they were formally taken into stock in April 1992. No.144 was seen at London Road, Silverhill on 8th April 1992. Paul Gainsbury

Unusual are the Iveco Daily midibuses with locally-built Phoenix bodywork. No.922, new in 1989, demonstrates the application of Coastline fleetname at Elm Lane, Havant. Adrian Churchill

Hampshire Bus took 10 Mercedes-Benz with Alexander bodywork in 1990. No.76 was found at Basing View, Basingstoke, with its name clearly indicated above the entrance. Peter Relf

THAMES TRANSIT GROUP

Thames Transit Ltd, Belgrave Road, Exeter, Devon, EX1 2AJ

Thames Transit started operations in Oxford on 7th March 1987 with a half-hourly coach service between Oxford and London marketed as 'Oxford Tube'. This has subsequently been increased in frequency and extended in London to Victoria. A minibus service in Oxford started from the same date and the network has been further extended since, notably through the acquisition of South Midland, from City of Oxford Motor Services in December 1988. The operating area now extends to Aylesbury, Eynsham and Witney.

Thames Transit forms part of the Transit Holdings group based at Exeter and inter-fleet changes frequently occur with Devon General and other operators in the group. The bulk of bus operation is with minibuses, though some larger vehicles are also used.

Blue Admiral started trading on 25th May 1991 as part of the Thames Transit group, covering local services in the Portsmouth area. This followed the introduction of Thames Transit operation in that area on 20th January 1991 as a result of the Monopolies and Mergers Commission directive to Southdown to divest itself of its Portsmouth operations. The fleet consists almost entirely of the ubiquitous Ford Transit/Mellor combination which characterises the Thames Transit group, although two former City of Portsmouth vehicles have also been acquired an Alexander-bodied Leyland Atlantean and one of the venerable open-top Leyland Titans with Metro-Cammell bodywork.

Red Admiral also started trading on 25th May 1991 as part of the Thames Transit group, covering out-of-town services in the Portsmouth area as well as local work at Gosport and Hilsea. Again, the fleet consists largely of the standard Ford Transit/Mellor machines although 43 Mercedes-Benz with Carlyle conversions joined the fleet in 1991 to replace the remaining conventional buses.

Operations are from a depot at Hilsea West for Red Admiral and a depot at Fareham, newly-opened in April 1991, for the Blue Admiral fleet.

Thames Transit operate the Oxford Tube service to London in direct competition with City of Oxford. The latest vehicles to join the fleet are six Volvo B10M-60s with Ikarus Blue Danube bodywork. Photographed in Ebury Street, London, is 23, the last of the 1991 delivery. Colin Lloyd

Forty-three Mercedes-Benz 811Ds with Carlyle bodywork arrived in 1991 to develop Red Admiral's presence in Portsmouth. Seen in the centre of that city while heading for Clanfield is 369, one of the first to arrive.
Ivor Norman

All 19 Iveco based minibuses in the Red Admiral operation have Robin Hood bodywork. New in 1988, No.972 arrived in Portsmouth in 1991 and is seen at Cosham in April 1992.
Adrian Churchill

Typical of the Thames Transit group is this Ford Transit VE6 with Mellor coachwork built in Rochdale, who have been a major supplier to this operator and part of the Plaxton/Henley group until early 1992. One of the 1987 delivery, 200 is seen in Portsmouth, where the once strong double-deck operation is now but a memory.
Ivor Norman

AUTOPOINT

B.P. Rodemark, Gardner Street, Herstmonceux, East Sussex, BN27 4LE

From small beginnings as a country minibus operator, Autopoint has expanded to a fleet of nearly 30 vehicles since deregulation in October 1986 operating a network of local bus services and contracts. Many of these are under contract to East Sussex County Council ranging as far as Lewes, Polegate, Hailsham, Heathfield, Haywards Heath, Rye and Hastings. This has resulted in additional full-size vehicles being taken into stock.

Vehicle policy has shown some enterprising trends, including the operation of Leyland Cubs, Dennis Lancets and others. Many vehicles have been re-registered with private AP marks originally issued in West Sussex. Fleet colours are white, dark blue and light blue and the fleet is based at Bodle Street.

Most of the Autopoint bus fleet comprises minibuses, such as 1241AP, a Mercedes-Benz L508D with Reeve Burgess conversion, new in 1982, seen in Eastbourne on 23rd January 1992 working a two-days-a-week service to Polegate. Many of the buses in this fleet have received local AP registrations. Terry Blackman

BEXHILL BUS COMPANY

M.J. Harmer, Wrestwood Road, Bexhill-on-Sea, East Sussex, TN40 2LP

The long-established coaching firm of Renown European was responsible for bailing out a consortium of former Maidstone & District employees which had set up a network of local services in December 1980. Operations were taken over in November 1981 and the combined fleet was operated from the present site at Westwood Road, Bexhill. In due course the Leyland Nationals involved were replaced by Leyland Panthers acquired from Eastbourne, now in turn ousted by Bristol REs from Hastings Buses.

Since October 1986 the bus side of the business has also undertaken tendered routes for East Sussex County Council in the rural area, and from September 1987 joint operation was introduced with Hastings & District on the main route between Hastings, Bexhill and Sidley.

The bus fleet is generally painted cream and blue, although the rural fleet carries the East Sussex County Council livery of dark green and yellow; the coaching operation remains identifiably separate in a white, grey, black and gold scheme. In addition to the main site at Bexhill a few vehicles are outstationed at Pevensey Bay.

Bexhill Bus Company, the stage side of Harmer's operation, has renewed most of its fleet with Bristol REs from Hastings & District, after several years of operating ex-Eastbourne Panthers. AHT212J is an RELL6L with Eastern Coach Works body new in 1971, originating within the Bristol group. Seen in Hastings on 11th March 1992 on a service co-ordinated with Hastings Buses, it has recently been numbered 412. Terry Blackman

BLUE SALOON

ABC Taxis (J. Lambley) Ltd, GB House, Westfield Road, Guildford, Surrey, GU1 1RR.

Blue Saloon has its origins with Blue Saloon Coaches of Guildford which started operations in 1924, although absorbed by the London Passenger Transport Board and Aldershot & District in 1938. Mr J Lambley, once a Blue Saloon driver, established a taxi business in Guildford in 1945 under the ABC name and in 1955 branched out to coach operation, obtaining the right to use the Blue Saloon name. Stage operations started on 1st March 1973 with a local Guildford service, gained after fierce competition for the licence with London Country and Tillingbourne Bus. The long-established business of Warner's Coaches, Milford was acquired on 1st August 1983.

As a result of discussions between the local operators and Surrey County Council a revised network was introduced in Guildford from 14th April 1985, and Blue Saloon has expanded its interests since deregulation including tendered operations in the Farnham area. An extensive programme of holidays, tours and excursions is also maintained under the name of GB Tours, reflecting former co-operation with Gastonia Coaches of Cranleigh. The fleet is painted in blue and white livery.

Blue Saloon operates local services in Guildford. Three Bristol LH6Ls with Eastern Coach Works bodies use the Hoppa-Shoppa marketing name, as typified by KPB881P. Ian Pringle

BYGONE BUSES

K.J. Morgan, Dye House, Biddenden, Kent, TN27 8AG

Bygone Buses, having taken over various coaching operations in the Maidstone area after its inception in February 1990 commenced a commercial network of services in Maidstone during September 1990. This has expanded gradually to incorporate some tendered work on behalf of Maidstone Borough Council and Kent County Council. Bygone now cover many of the rural services formerly worked by Boro'line Maidstone, together with Kent County Council route 333 on Sundays from Maidstone to Canterbury.

The bus services are normally resourced from the Leyland Nationals and Leopards, with occasional cameo operations by the Routemaster. A Bristol VRT and one of the prototype Leyland Titans add spice to the scene.

Most buses are painted in a red livery and carry appropriate names.

NHG732P was the first Titan to be built and started life in evaluatory service with London Transport. It has had a number of owners since and was bought by Bygone Buses in 1990. It was photographed at Chart Sutton in June 1992. David Harman

Bygone Buses has developed a network of routes in the Maidstone area since the late summer of 1990, contributing to pressure on Boro'line Maidstone. GAE371N, a dual-door Leyland National of 1974 now owned by Turner's, carries the mainly red livery of most of the fleet. Terry Blackman

GKL826N is a Bristol VRT2 with Eastern Coach Works body acquired from Maidstone & District in 1990 and now competing alongside routes of its original owner. Named 'Red Rooster', it is seen at All Saints' Church. Terry Blackman

COASTAL COACHES

P.H.Jenkins, 23 Corsica Road, Seaford, East Sussex, BN25 1BD

Coastal Coaches commenced coach operation in the Seaford area during 1988, working in close association with Eastbourne Buses. In October 1990 an East Sussex County Council contract was gained for route 346 between Silverhill (Hastings) and Pett, and two Leyland Nationals have been purchased to support this operation.

Vehicles have operated in as-acquired colours, though a corporate livery is about to be introduced. The buses are generally parked at the Hastings Buses depot at Silverhill.

Coastal Coaches have two Leyland Nationals for a weekday service from Hastings to Pett and a Sunday service from Hastings to Tenterden (Ashford in the summer), both under contract to ESCC. PJJ343S was acquired from East Kent in 1991 and was seen at Ore on 8th April 1992 after receiving the livery of its new owner. It has since been re-registered. Paul Gainsbury

CHILTERN QUEENS

Chiltern Queens Ltd, Greenmore, Woodcote, Oxfordshire, RG8 0RP

Chiltern Queens was formed in July 1955 as the successor to Kemp's Motor Services Ltd, also of Woodcote. Three new AEC Reliances were soon purchased together with secondhand coaches, and subsequent vehicles have included Albion, Maudslay and Tilling-Stevens. Chiltern Queens developed a strong bias towards AEC Reliances, both new and acquired. Now, however, Leyland Leopards and Volvos are acquiring a foothold with the gradual decline of AEC availability.

Three main services are operated from Reading together with a Henley Town Service and a number of occasional rural services.

Two Mercedes-Benz 811D reside in the Chiltern Queens fleet, principally for use on the tendered services. Photographed at Reading is F986TTF, an Optare StarRider. The other vehicle is fitted with an Alexander AM body. Malcolm King

National Bus ordered many Duple Dominant-bodied Leyland Leopards for their subsidiaries, many with the express doorway to attract the government bus-grant. Chiltern Queens have several examples which were new to City of Oxford. Seen at its new base is RFC10T. Terry Blackman

DONSWAY

R.J. Harris, London Road, Dunkirk, Faversham, Kent, ME13 9LQ

Donsway was involved in local bus operation since early in the 1980s, and has developed this interest through tendered operations from Kent County Council since deregulation. There is also a significant presence in local contract operations.

Most vehicles are in orange and red livery, and some carry 'Private Enterprise' names to reflect the spirit of the bus operations, which are usually covered by the Leyland National and bus-grant coaches.

Donsway has participated in local bus operation for a decade now. Starting with an ex-Maidstone Borough Council Bedford, the current dedicated bus is THX235S, a Leyland National acquired from London Buses in 1989, seen in Faversham on 8th March 1991 still in London Buses red. Terry Blackman

EAST SURREY

East Surrey, Tilburstow Hill, South Godstone, RH9 8JZ

East Surrey Buses have developed a higher profile in bus work since de-regulation, and in recent times have gained some significant contracts from both Kent and Surrey County Councils. These are in addition to expanding commercial initiatives. The original fleet, largely based on Bedford chassis, has been updated with Optare StarRiders, an Optare MetroRider, CVE Omnis and a Dennis Dart. A small number of coaches are also operated in private hire work.

Fleet livery is orange and cream and the vehicles are based at South Godstone.

The East Grinstead-Tunbridge Wells routes 239/291 are tendered to Wealden Beeline and East Surrey by Kent CC, with support from East and West Sussex CCs. Both use new Dennis Darts with Wadham Stringer bodywork for the majority of workings. Here, the East Surrey example picks up at 'The Hare', Langton Green, inbound for Tunbridge Wells on a fine morning in June 1992. David Harman

FARLEIGH COACHES

D.R. Smith, St Peter's Works, Hall Road, Wouldham, Kent, ME1 3XL

Farleigh Coaches commenced local coaching operations in August 1982, though not using that trading name until later. Bus operations were introduced at deregulation and although a weekday evening contract between Maidstone and Borough Green has since passed elsewhere, the main service 58 between Maidstone and Trottiscliffe remains. This is notable having been introduced commercially to replace a Maidstone & District facility, although it is now covered by Kent County Council support. The usual vehicle is now the former London Buses Leyland National with a former Western National Bedford and a former East Kent AEC Swift as reserves.

Fleet livery is basically white.

Farleigh Coaches use this ex-Western National Bedford YRQ with Duple bodywork on their KCC contract service between Maidstone and the Trottiscliffe area. Here it loads at Maidstone Queen's Monument before departing on what was originally at Maidstone & District service. Terry Blackman

FUGGLES

Fuggles of Benenden Ltd, Bramley Orchard, Cranbrook Road, Benenden, Kent, TN17 4EU

Fuggles traces its origin back to the late 1920s and the establishment of a garage in the country village in 1927. The firm passed into new management during the summer of 1989 and the original trading name was reinstated after a period during which the limited company name of Penjon had been used for official purposes.

Stage services started in June 1980 and the company subsequently built up a network of services in the rural area bordered by Maidstone, Tunbridge Wells and Tenterden. Many of these are operated on a commercial basis. The recession has meant that most of these have since come under Kent County Council auspices, and a number have been lost to other operators in the 1992 tendering round. However, a Kent Karrier service in the Ashford area was gained, and an Omni midibus is due to join the fleet for this purpose.

Fleet livery is deep red and cream with pale red relief, and the fleet is housed in a new depot at Apple Pie Farm, Benenden.

Fuggles' bus fleet is based on vehicles from the local major operators. SKN911R is one of two Leyland Nationals with dual-purpose seating received from Hastings & District in 1989, Bristol REs going in the opposite direction in part-exchange. Here it is seen at Rye on an ESCC contracted service worked by Fuggles on Saturdays and by Rye Coaches for the rest of the week. Richard Lewis

HANTS & SUSSEX
SOUTHERN MOTORWAYS

B.S. Williams Ltd, Hollybank House, Emsworth, Hampshire, PO10 7LN

The original Hants & Sussex Motor Services Ltd had a chequered history between its formation in 1937 and cessation in 1954. The proprietor, Mr Basil Williams, formed a new company in his own name in October 1955, purchasing Glider & Blue Motor Services Ltd of Bishop's Waltham & Fareham in December 1959. In 1962 the fleetname Southern Motorways was adopted. The coach interests of White Heather Transport Ltd, Southsea were acquired in 1977 and a new company was formed on 1st October 1977, White Heather Travel, to take over the fleet of seven coaches. Victoria Coaches, Southsea was a further acquisition in May 1979. White Heather Travel was sold in June 1984.

The Glider & Blue section was sold to Solent Blue Line, an associate of Southern Vectis, on 1st October 1987.

The residual services fall into two groups. One group is based on Emsworth, trading as Hants & Sussex; the other is based at Midhurst, using the Southern Motorways name. Vehicles carry a livery of red, cream and black (coaches are cream and red) and are based at Southleigh Farm, Southleigh Road, Emsworth.

Hants & Sussex have in recent years developed a penchant for former London Merlins and Swifts. DPD502J is one of the latter type new to London Country with MCW bodywork and carries its age well in this view. Andrew Jarosz

HAVEN COACHES

D P Mulpeter & R H Cutbush, 6 Murrey Avenue, Newhaven, East Sussex, BN9 9SE

D P Mulpeter and G P Marshall commenced trading on 29th July 1991 with an hourly crew-operated route on weekdays between Newhaven and Brighton. Two months later the frequency was doubled and journeys extended to Chyngton Estate, Seaford.

During January 1992 Marshall was replaced in the partnership by R H Cutbush, who had applied for authorization the previous autumn as Newhaven & District Motor Services. The services were further revised on 27th January, and on 17th April Sunday operations were added, followed by a Haven Hopper service on 4th May.

Much of the fleet is based on former London vehicles, though a former Maidstone Leyland Atlantean was used during the autumn of 1991, since replaced by another Leyland Atlantean originating with Northern General. The fleet is based at Newhaven Industrial Estate.

Haven Coaches introduced a conductor-operated service between Newhaven and Brighton in the summer of 1991 and have expanded since. Routemaster WLT960 demonstrates what is probably the southernmost operation of a Routemaster in England in this view. E.C. Churchill

INLAND TRAVEL

H A P Roffey, Flimwell Service Station, London Road, Flimwell, East Sussex, TN5 7PG

Inland Travel has for many years operated a high-quality coaching fleet in the middle of the Wealden countryside, contracting to major tour operators as well as providing some vehicles on local contracts. Prestige vehicles are frequently hired in on a short-term basis during the summer months for Continental operations.

From 29th March 1992 Inland Travel has gained a small amount of tendered bus work for Kent County Council in the Tunbridge Wells area.

Fleet livery is white; some vehicles carry either blue or red and orange relief.

A recent arrival on the local bus scene is Inland Travel of Flimwell, who acquired a group of KCC services at the end of March 1992. Leyland National VKE569S is back in its home county, having been new to Maidstone & District before passing to Hastings & District and East Midland. This view was taken at Rye Station. Terry Blackman

77

KENT COACH TOURS

D.C. Farmer, 98 Ellingham Way, Ashford, Kent, TN23 2NF

From October 1986 Kent Coach Tours secured a Kent County Council tender for a service between Ashford and Faversham, with some journeys extended to Oare and Luddenham. In March 1988 a local Ashford service was added, followed by a service from Folkestone, through Alkham, to Dover in April 1990. A further local service in Ashford was introduced commercially in November 1990.

Having lost the Faversham service in March 1992 and with a possibility of also losing the tendered local Ashford route, Kent Coach Tours registered the latter commercially and introduced an enhanced timetable coupling it to the existing commercial service. However, this was withdrawn two months later. All of these operations are normally worked by the Leyland Nationals and the Eastern Coach Works-bodied Leyland Leopards.

Kent Coach Tours bought two of these Leyland Leopard/Eastern Coach Works vehicles in 1990, though EBD181X is now the sole survivor following tendering losses. The blind in this view at Canterbury Bus Station appears to cover most eventualities. Malcolm King

MARCHWOOD MOTORWAYS

Marchwood Motorways (Southampton) Ltd, 200 Salisbury Road, Totton, Hants, SO4 3ZP

Marchwood Motorways was formed in October 1955 by D H Osborne and C I Arnold to operate contract services in and around the oil refinery of Fawley. A pair of Bedford OBs, A Crossley and a Leyland Cheetah formed the initial fleet. Work in the Haverfordwest and Milford Haven area of South Wales was also undertaken, though this has now ceased. Various small operators in the Southampton area have been acquired the most recent being Osgoods of Totton in 1972. De-regulation saw the introduction of the Totton-Link hail and ride service which used two Iveco minibuses.

The first franchised bus service in the UK started in 1988 when Solent Blue Line contracted out two routes for which several Leyland Nationals were transferred to the Marchwood fleet. Subsequent new vehicle for Marchwood, including Optare Deltas and Dennis Darts, are also in Solent Blue Line livery.

The company gained its present name in 1989. In addition to the PCV fleet there is a large fleet of taxis and self-drive hire vehicles. Vehicles are in a livery of red and cream or white and are housed at Totton.

No.214 is one of two Carlyle bodied Dennis Darts in the Marchwood fleet, this one being the longer of the two. Service 52 is operated as a franchise from Solent Blue Line, hence the livery, and this photo was taken at Bishops Waltham. A. Gilmour

MERCURY PASSENGER SERVICES

S.L. Edgecombe & R.H. Hall, 31 Nursery Gardens, Hoo St Werburgh, Kent, ME3 9BN

Mercury Passenger Services has gained a number of Kent County Council contracts in the Maidstone and Medway areas since the end of March 1991, consolidating these with some commercial operations. Services extend along the Hoo peninsula to the north and as far south as Goudhurst in the Kent countryside. Proposals are under discussion to extend this network with further rural services.

Vehicles have generally operated in as-acquired liveries, but a maroon livery has recently been introduced for the former London Buses Optare-bodied City Pacers.

Both Leyland Nationals in the Mercury Passenger Services fleet originated from East Kent in 1991. PJJ342S, still in East Kent colours, is a 10.3m example, found on layover in Maidstone between journeys on the KCC contract service through the hopfields to Goudhurst. Terry Blackman

NU-VENTURE

Nu-Venture Coaches Ltd, 86 Mill Hall, Aylesford, Maidstone, Kent, ME20 7JN

The long-established local coaching form of Nu-Venture has operated a number of contracts for Kent County Council since deregulation, and has supplemented these by commercial operations to the west of Maidstone, sometimes taking advantage of what would otherwise be light running between tendered work and the home base.

Most of the fleet currently carries white livery, though the Leyland Tiger coaches have received red and blue stripes to augment this.

Nu-Venture have three Peugeot-Talbot Pullmans which provide most of the cover for their bus operations. G75TKN was new in 1990 and has dual-purpose seating. This view at Maidstone Queen's Monument in May 1991 shows operation on the KCC Sunday contract to Tenterden which had been gained one month previously. Terry Blackman

POYNTER'S

R.J. & B.J. Poynter, Sunray, Churchfield Way, Wye, Ashford, Kent, TN25 5EQ

Poynter's have developed an interest in Kent County Council tendered work on rural routes in the Ashford and Canterbury areas since deregulation. However, the spring 1992 tendering round deprived them of their work on the Ashford to Aldington service, and bus work is now confined to the service between Canterbury and Charing. There is a strong presence on local works and schools contracts.

The fleet carries a livery of cream with yellow and orange.

Poynter's acquired two short Leyland Nationals from Crosville Wales in mid-1991 for their KCC contracts based on Canterbury. HMA562T basks in the sun at the bus station. Malcolm King

PRIORY COACHES

Cyril Cowdrey Ltd, Quay Lane, Gosport, Hampshire, PO12 4LJ

In the mid-1920s James Dyer, a Gosport schoolmaster, began a local service using a Model T Ford. In 1953 he sold his stage carriage interests to Provincial. These included the routes from Gosport Ferry to Kings Road and to Albermarle Avenue. He retained some Bedford OBs and an Austin to run the private hire work as Priory Coaches from his address at 1 Priory Road.

In 1956 his nephew, Cyril Cowdrey, joined the company and eventually acquired it from his uncle. The first continental tour was undertaken in 1966, this in addition to an expanding excursions and tour programme at home.

Following de-regulation in 1986, a number of tendered contracts were secured from Hampshire County Council, reintroducing stage operation for the first time since 1953. In 1988 the two-coach business of ABC Coaches was taken over, though the livery is still retained. The garage and office is in Quay Lane and there is a travel office in Royan Gardens.

RAMBLER

Mrs M. & C. Rowland and J. Goodwin, West Ridge Manor, Whitworth Road,
St Leonards-on-Sea, East Sussex, TN37 7PZ

The business was founded in 1924 by R.G. Rowland. Local bus operations started with an East Sussex County Council service between Bexhill and Hooe from 1980 to 1982. Since May 1986 Rambler has operated several journeys of the East Sussex County Rider scheme in the Battle and Bexhill areas, and from July 1987 took over a cross-Hastings service between St Leonards and Hollington. In October 1990 this was lost, but simultaneously a new Sunday service covering part of the route was gained and a commercial service in Hastings began. From September 1991 the coastal service between Hastings, Fairlight and Rye commenced under tender. Vehicles used on these services carry a Ramblerbus name.

Fleet livery is green, black and cream with pale green relief. The present garage was opened in May 1980 and the head office moved there in January 1990.

RYE COACHES

P.F. White-Hide & K.M. Bowen, Harbour Road, Rye, Kent, TN31 7TE

Rye Coaches entered local bus operation in October 1990 when the Monday to Friday contract for East Sussex County Council route 312, between Rye and Tenterden, was gained together with occasional day journeys on other rural routes. Some school work, previously operated by Hastings Buses, was also secured in September 1991 and further work that commenced on 29th March 1992 has been obtained from Kent County Council.

Vehicles are painted in silver and blue, although earlier acquisitions are in cream with brown and orange stripes. A yard is used at Rye Harbour for local operations.

Priory of Gosport use this 25-seat Mercedes with coach-seated Reeve Burgess body for tendered bus services. It is seen in Fareham bus station working route 34A, which is a tendered service for Hampshire County Council.
A. Gilmour

Chiefly noted for their extensive coach operations based in Hastings, Rambler have ventured into a corner of the local bus market since deregulation. Having lost their weekday ESCC contract in October 1990, a commercial route was introduced alongside Hastings Buses. WNH52W, a Bedford YMQS, stands at the Hollington Tesco superstore on this service.
Terry Blackman

The deregistration of school services in the Rye area by Hastings Buses in September 1991 brought Rye Coaches onto such work. Former South Yorkshire Leyland Atlantean/Roe CWG757V was seen in Waites Lane, Fairlight in April 1992. Terry Blackman

SAFEGUARD

Safeguard Coaches Ltd, Friary Bus Station, Commercial Road, Guildford, Surrey, GU2 5TH

The fleet originated in a charabanc operation started in 1924 by Arthur Newman, a local coal merchant and haulage contractor. A stage service in Guildford commenced in 1927.

For many years Safeguard pursued a vehicle policy based on the locally-produced Dennis chassis, though the current fleet has Leylands in predominance. More recently, Farnham Coaches was acquired together with five Setras, and other vehicles have since been painted into Farnham Coaches livery and gained private index marks. In addition to local services, the company operates a stage service between Aldershot and Camberley during the week and school services in the surrounding area.

The bus livery is dark red and cream while coaches are painted cream, red and grey. The garage is at Ridgemount Garage, Guildford Park. Farnham Coaches vehicles are kept at Odiham Road, Ewshot, Farnham.

Safeguard operate four Leyland Lynx, all delivered new from Lillyhall, the first pair having the stepped floor layout, while the latter pair feature the ramped floor option. All four have the Leyland TL11 engine fitted. E51MMT is seen on Guildford local service G4 at Park Barn, Guildford, in August 1992.
Ian Pringle

Two Mercedes-Benz minibuses arrived in 1986. Both bodied by Reeve Burgess, one with coach seating is based on a van conversion, while the other, D159HML, has a minibus body constructed on a chassis-cab base.
Ian Pringle

SMITH'S

W.H.V and Mrs V. Smith, 59 Staplehurst Road, Sittingbourne, Kent, ME10 2NY

Following the relaxation of licensing regulations in October 1980 Smith's Coaches started a commuter service between Sheerness, Sittingbourne and London which now operates under the 'Concorde' banner. Local bus operations started in the spring of 1986 when a pre-deregulation pilot batch of tenders was offered by Kent County Council. Leyland Nationals were purchased in 1987 to replace the original bus-grant Ford coaches. In November 1989 Smith's Coaches stepped in to take over the Kent County Council routes between Sheerness and Sittingbourne surrendered by Lambkin Coaches and also commenced a weekday-evening, tendered operation of the local services on the Isle of Sheppey. Market-day services to Maidstone and Canterbury also form part of the business.

Most vehicles are in grey, black and white (some also with red) and the fleet is based at the licensed address.

Smith, Sittingbourne was an early beneficiary of KCC tendering in the mid-1980s, and subsequently bought secondhand Leyland Nationals for these operations. ODL885R came from Southern Vectis, and is smartly turned-out in this view on a Sittingbourne service. Malcolm King

SUSSEX BUS

Sussex Bus Ltd, 11 June Close, Bognor Regis, West Sussex, PO21 4UH

Sussex Bus was founded by John Belson of Partridge Green, Sussex, in the summer of 1985, to operate a number of bus services into Brighton from the rural area to the north-west. Contracts were soon gained from West Sussex County Council taking vehicles to Haywards Heath, Horsham and Worthing at weekends. From the outset the fleet has been characterised by vehicles carrying advertising for the local Evening Argus newspaper, whose colours inspired the distinctive red and white livery.

In January 1989 a substantial block of West Sussex contract services were obtained in the Chichester area following withdrawal by Yellowline Coaches, and the bulk of the company's work now focuses in this area. During the summer of 1989 there was also an open-top circular service from Chichester to Bognor Regis, Littlehampton, Arundel and back to Chichester.

The Sussex Bus fleet has seen regular change since the last edition of this book, most of the fleet having been replaced. SJA351K is one of a brace of Bristol RELL6Ls with Marshall bodywork acquired in 1989 and was seen on the Hayling Island local route in September 1991. Terry Blackman

THANET BUS

G.C. Chisholm & R.J. Booth, 81 South Eastern Road, Ramsgate, Kent, CT11 9QE

Thanet Bus has developed from local bus operations introduced by Chisholm in the Isle of Thanet during 1988. At one stage these led to keen competition with East Kent, although the two parties both withdrew to a compatible position in March 1990. Subsequently Thanet Bus gained Kent County Council contracts covering former East Kent work from Ramsgate to the westerly villages, as well as the weekday evening contracts for local services within Thanet and to Canterbury; the local work is also undertaken on Sundays.

To a large extent the original midibuses have now been supplanted by a variety of acquired single-deckers, chiefly Leyland Nationals, most operating in a white and red livery. These vehicles cover a range of contracts during the daytime in addition to their major presence on the island services during weekday evenings.

Thanet Bus have upgraded from minibuses to full-size vehicles as they have developed their involvement in local bus work, especially since gaining important evening and Sunday contracts from KCC in 1991. Leyland National NEN963R came from Cambus and was found at Ramsgate Harbour on the daytime service round the island to Westgate on 23rd March 1991. Brian Weeden

Two Dennis Darts with Carlyle bodywork arrived in the spring of 1991, though one has subsequently been released. H851NOC stands at Canterbury Bus Station on a Sunday working once the preserve of East Kent, and on which the latter has just reintroduced a commercial service. Richard Lewis

TILLINGBOURNE

Tillingbourne Bus Co Ltd, Littlemead Estate, Alford Road, Cranleigh, Surrey, GU6 8ND

Tillingbourne Bus Company dates back to 1924 when Mr G Trice, a country carrier based in Chilworth near Guildford, started motor bus operation under the name of Tillingbourne Valley Services. A Guildford town service started in 1931 and lasted for 40 years. A limited company was formed in 1935 and since 1972 has run under its present title.

Activities extended into Sussex in 1972 when North Downs Rural Transport ceased, Tillingbourne taking the Horsham and Rusper circular service. A separate company, Tillingbourne (Sussex) Ltd, was formed in May 1974 to administer this operation. Tillingbourne expanded again in 1981 when services in the Orpington and East Croydon areas were taken over from Orpington & District. These were handed over to Metrobus in September 1983. The Surrey Hills and Sussex Weald services were revised in November 1982 following the takeover of Tony McCann Coaches of Forest Green.

The present network consists of a variety of services in the Guildford, Cranleigh, Fleet, Farnborough, Horsham, Reigate and Crawley areas. Fleet livery is blue, white and yellow and the main garage is at Cranleigh with a subsidiary site at Foundry Close Industrial Estate, Horsham.

Stalwarts of the service bus fleet are the Leyland Tiger buses. B877OLJ, showing off its Duple Dominant body, is seen in Horsham while working the North Heath Circular. David Harman

Now the oldest vehicle in the Tillingbourne fleet, ODV404W also has the distinction of being the only AEC remaining. Acquired from Metrobus in 1991, it carries the deeper-screened version of the Duple Dominant body introduced as the Mark 2. It is seen at Holmbury St Mary.
Ian Pringle

A pair of Dennis Dorchester buses joined the fleet new in 1983. Fitted with the Wadham Stringer Vanguard body, the first of the pair, FOD942Y, is seen at Horsham in June 1992.
David Harman

New arrival with Tillingbourne is E364NEG. Based on a 1987 Volvo B10M chassis, it has been rebodied with the latest Countybus design from Northern Counties. It is seen in Shalford in August 1992.
Ian Pringle

TOWN & AROUND

Town & Around (Folkestone) Ltd, 5 Thanet Gardens, Folkestone, Kent, CT19 6DE

In October 1986 Robert Miller started a local service in Folkestone between Holywell Avenue and Broadmead Village. The network was expanded in March 1988 with the acquisition of Kent County Council contracts for weekday routes 558 and 559 between Hythe and Canterbury through Stelling Minnis and a Sunday route from Folkestone to Maidstone, although these Kent County Council services were lost on re-tendering from 1st April 1990. Instead, Kent County Council route 593 from Dover (Western Heights) to Martin in St Margaret's Bay was gained from 1st April 1990. The present company was authorised in November 1989 although Miller had used the trading name since inception.

The fleet is in a livery of white with blue skirt and light blue stripes.

The enthusiast-operated Town & Around concern at Folkestone has found a mutually-agreeable existence alongside East Kent. The original and main route between Holywell and Broadmead Village received this Leyland Swift with Wadham Stringer bodywork during the summer of 1991. Here it is seen at Holywell Avenue on 20th July 1991, driven by the proprietor.
John Grubb

WARREN

Warren Coaches (Kent & Sussex) Ltd, High Street, Ticehurst, East Sussex, TN5 7AN

Warren Coaches of Ticehurst (associated with the Tenterden company of the same name) has been the longest-standing of coach operators in the Weald of Kent, tracing its ancestry back more than sixty years. Until October 1990, operations were chiefly concerned with private hire, contract and excursion work. Then the company made a successful bid for East Sussex County Council routes 254 and 256, and these are now worked between Hawkhurst and Tunbridge Wells.

Most vehicles carry a yellow livery with blue and red stripes, though there are some differences in application.

Warren of Ticehurst is another operator to have diversified from coach operation into local bus services, taking over the Hawkhurst to Tunbridge Wells corridor in October 1990. THX146S originated with London Buses and is seen on a service to the High Weald. Paul Gainsbury

School traffic on these services is catered for by two Bristol VRTs with Eastern Coach Works bodies acquired from M&D during 1990. GKL825N stands at Tunbridge Wells War Memorial on the main route to Hawkhurst on 15th November 1990. Terry Blackman

WEALDEN BEELINE

Wealden PSV Ltd, Badsell Road, Five Oak Green, Kent, TN12 6QY

Wealden PSV has developed an increasing presence in local bus operation in recent years. In addition to a school service between Wateringbury and Paddock Wood, local authority tendered operations are run between Tunbridge Wells and Groombridge; Tunbridge Wells and East Grinstead, joint with East Surrey; and for Tonbridge local services, including the Hildenborough commuter rail link. Absorption of Beeline, Southborough early in 1989 led to involvement in the Tunbridge Wells to Heathfield service, with some departures operating under East Sussex County Council auspices.

The fleet composition has included a number of unusual vehicles transferred from the associated dealing firm, Wealden PSV Sales, and from time to time machines from this arm are found in service. The livery is two shades of green with cream relief.

Retendered KCC contracts in the Tunbridge Wells area at the end of March 1992 led to Wealden-Beeline securing work on routes 239 and 291 to Tunbridge Wells in conjunction with East Surrey Motors. Ex-demonstrator Dennis Dart/Wadham Stringer J459JOW represents Wealden's contribution to the operation at East Grinstead Station in June 1992. David Harman

WESTBUS

Westbus (UK) Ltd, Travel House, Hunter Avenue, Willesborough, Ashford, Kent, TN24 0HB

The Australian firm of Westbus purchased the Swinard, Ashford operation in December 1986, adding ADP Travel Services Ltd of Hounslow in January 1987. The two operations are now managed as one. Swinards had a long-established history in local coaching but bus operation started in March 1988 when a batch of Ashford area services was gained under Kent County Council tender. These included rural routes to Smarden, Hastingleigh, Brabourne Lees, Westwell and a Sunday local service. In March 1989 the route from Faversham to Whitstable was added together with local services from Faversham to Selling and Doddington. Westbus are also responsible for the Thursday route between Mersham and Folkestone, and from 1st April 1990 took over routes between Ashford and Lydd across the Romney Marsh, between Hythe and Canterbury via Stelling Minnis, and the evening service between Folkestone and Lydd. From 29th March 1992 the service from Ashford to Faversham was gained, though at the expense of the routes to Smarden, Hastingleigh, Brabourne Lees, Westwell and the Ashford local Sunday service. The Hounslow operation, meanwhile, continues to focus on high-quality coaching work and airport transfers in the London area.

Fleet livery is deep red and apricot, and is based at the Willesborough address and at Spring Grove Road, Hounslow.

The Australian-controlled Westbus company took over the long-established coach operations of Swinard, Ashford at the end of 1986, and has shown a lively interest in KCC contract work since. The company received three 1980 Leyland National 2 buses surplus to the requirements of Sheffield United in 1990/1. RFS586V is on the KCC contract route to Hythe. Malcolm King

ALDER VALLEY Fleet List

131	NRD131M	Leyland National 1151/1R/0402		B49F	1973	Ex Thames Valley & Aldershot, 1986
141	NRD141M	Leyland National 1151/1R/0402		B49F	1973	Ex Thames Valley & Aldershot, 1986

175-232

Leyland National 11351/1R   B49F   1974-75   Ex Thames Valley & Aldershot, 1986

175	TBL175M	201	HPK503N	215	KPA366P	220	KPA371P	228	KPA379P
179	UMO179N	203	HPK505N	217	KPA368P	223	KPA374P	232	KPA383P
180	UMO180N	214	KPA365P	218	KPA369P	227	KPA378P		

236	KPA387P	Leyland National 11351A/1R		B49F	1976	Ex Thames Valley & Aldershot, 1986
237	KPA388P	Leyland National 11351A/1R		B49F	1976	Ex Thames Valley & Aldershot, 1986
238	KPA389P	Leyland National 11351A/1R		B49F	1976	Ex Thames Valley & Aldershot, 1986
240	LPF598P	Leyland National 11351/1R/SC		DP45F	1976	Ex Thames Valley & Aldershot, 1986
247	LPF605P	Leyland National 11351/1R/SC		B49F	1976	Ex Thames Valley & Aldershot, 1986

253-273

Leyland National 11351A/1R   B49F   1976-78   Ex Thames Valley & Aldershot, 1986

253	NPJ474R	255	NPJ476R	259	NPJ480R	264	NPJ485R	272	TPE149S
254	NPJ475R	256	NPJ477R	261	NPJ482R	271	TPE148S	273	TPE150S

276	TPE169S	Leyland National 11351A/1R		DP45F	1976	Ex Thames Valley & Aldershot, 1986
279	VPF295S	Leyland National 11351A/1R		DP45F	1976	Ex Thames Valley & Aldershot, 1986

401-410

Renault-Dodge S46   Northern Counties   B22F   1987

401	E401EPE	403	E403EPE	405	E405EPE	408	E408EPE	410	E410EPE
402	E402EPE	404	E404EPE	406	E406EPE	409	E409EPE		

411-420

Renault-Dodge S56   Northern Counties   B27F   1987-88

411	E411EPE	413	E413EPE	415	E415EPE	418	E418EPE	420	E420EPE
412	E412EPE	414	E414EPE	417	E417EPE	419	E419EPE		

469-476

Iveco Daily 49.10   Robin Hood   B21F   1986

469	D469WPM	471	D471WPM	473	D473WPM	475	D475WPM	476	D476WPM
470	D470WPM	472	D472WPM	474	D474WPM				

477	E201EPB	Iveco Daily 49.10	Robin Hood	B25F	1987
478	E202EPB	Iveco Daily 49.10	Robin Hood	B25F	1987
479	E203EPB	Iveco Daily 49.10	Robin Hood	B25F	1987
480	E204EPB	Iveco Daily 49.10	Robin Hood	B25F	1987
485	F695OPA	Iveco Daily 49.10	Carlyle Dailybus	B23F	1988
490	F700OPA	Iveco Daily 49.10	Carlyle Dailybus	B23F	1988
491	F701OPA	Iveco Daily 49.10	Carlyle Dailybus	B23F	1988
494	G864BPD	Iveco Daily 49.10	Carlyle Dailybus	B23F	1989
503	AAA503C	Dennis Loline III	Weymann	H39/29F	1964

601-626

Bristol VRT/SL3/6LXB   Eastern Coach Works   H43/31F   1980   Ex Thames Valley & Aldershot, 1986

602	CJH142V	611	GGM81W	615	GGM85W	622	KKK888V	625	GGM105W
605	CJH145V	612	GGM82W	616	GGM86W	623	GGM103W	626	GGM106W
610	GGM80W	613	GGM83W	621	KKK887V	624	GGM104W		

754	YPJ204Y	Leyland Tiger TRCTL11/3R	Plaxton Paramount 3500	C50F	1983	Ex The Bee Line, 1992

782-789

Volvo B10M-61   Jonckheere Jubilee P50   C53F   1989   Ex Berks Bucks, 1992

782	F772OJH	783	F773OJH	786	F756OJH	788	F758OJH	789	F759OJH

801	K801CAN	Leyland Lynx LX2R11V18Z4S	Leyland	B51F	1992
802	K802CAN	Leyland Lynx LX2R11V18Z4S	Leyland	B51F	1992

942-981

Bristol VRT/SL3/6LXB   Eastern Coach Works   H43/31F   1977-80   Ex Thames Valley & Aldershot, 1986

942	PPM903R	953	VPF283S	966	WJM826T	969	WJM829T	979	CJH119V
950	TPE156S	964	WJM824T	967	WJM827T	972	WJM832T	980	CJH120V
951	VPF281S	965	WJM825T	968	WJM828T	977	CJH117V	981	CJH121V
952	VPF282S								

983	CJH123V	Bristol VRT/SL3/6LXB	Eastern Coach Works	DPH41/25F	1979	Ex Thames Valley & Aldershot, 1986
1125	RPB955X	Leyland Leopard PSU3G/4R	Eastern Coach Works B51	C49F	1982	Ex Thames Valley & Aldershot, 1986
1128	WPD28Y	Leyland Leopard PSU3G/4R	Eastern Coach Works B51	C49F	1982	Ex Thames Valley & Aldershot, 1986
1185	WJM805T	Leyland Leopard PSU3E/4R	Plaxton Supreme IV	C46F	1978	Ex Thames Valley & Aldershot, 1986
1206	E206EPB	Hestair Duple 425	Duple 425	C57F	1987	
1207	E207EPB	Hestair Duple 425	Duple 425	C57F	1987	
1208	E208EPB	Hestair Duple 425	Duple 425	C57F	1987	
1298	SGS504W	Leyland Tiger TRCTL11/3R	Plaxton Supreme IV	C50F	1981	Ex Thames Valley & Aldershot, 1986
1299	XGS762X	Leyland Tiger TRCTL11/3R	Plaxton Supreme IV	C50F	1981	Ex Thames Valley & Aldershot, 1986
1502	YPJ502Y	Leyland Olympian ONTL11/2R	Eastern Coach Works	CH45/28F	1983	Ex Thames Valley & Aldershot, 1986

THE BEE LINE Fleet List

102	C322RPE	Ford Transit 190	Carlyle	B16F	1986	

161-182

Mercedes-Benz 609D   Robin Hood   B20F   1987   175 ex London Buslines, 1990

161	E457CGM	167	E463CGM	171	E467CGM	176	E472CGM	180	E476CGM
162	E458CGM	168	E464CGM	173	E469CGM	177	E473CGM	181	E477CGM
165	E461CGM	169	E465CGM	174	E470CGM	178	E474CGM	182	E478CGM
166	E462CGM	170	E466CGM	175	E471CGM	179	E475CGM		

302-317

Leyland National 1151/1R/0402   B49F   1973-74   Ex Thames Valley & Aldershot, 1986

302	NRD134M	311	NRD152M	313	NRD154M	316	NRD159M	317	NRD160M
304	NRD136M	311	NRD155M						

326-352

Leyland National 11351/1R   B49F   1974-75   Ex Thames Valley & Aldershot, 1986

326	TBL170M	336	GPC736N	348	KPA362P	347	KPA360P	350	KPA376P
329	TBL174M	338	GPJ894N	342	HPK501N	349	KPA370P	352	KPA381P
331	UMO178N								

355-365

Leyland National 11351A/1R   B49F   1976-78   Ex Thames Valley & Aldershot, 1986
359 ex Alder Valley, 1990

355	NPJ473R	359	NPJ484R	363	TPE164S	364	TPE165S	365	TPE167S
358	PPM896R	362	TPE162S						

372	LPF599P	Leyland National 11351/1R/SC		DP21FL	1976	Ex Thames Valley & Aldershot, 1986
374	LPF601P	Leyland National 11351/1R/SC		DP45F	1976	Ex Thames Valley & Aldershot, 1986
375	LPF606P	Leyland National 11351/1R/SC		B45F	1976	Ex Thames Valley & Aldershot, 1986
377	NPJ471R	Leyland National 11351A/1R		DP21FL	1977	Ex Thames Valley & Aldershot, 1986
381	LPF602P	Leyland National 11351/1R/SC		B45F	1976	Ex Thames Valley & Aldershot, 1986

516-560

Bristol VRT/SL3/6LXB   Eastern Coach Works   H43/31F   1978-80   Ex Thames Valley & Aldershot, 1986

518	TPE155S	524	WJM821T	532	CJH143V	539	GGM89W	559	GGM84W
521	VPF286S	525	WJM830T	533	CJH144V	540	GGM90W	560	GGM107W
523	WJM819T	526	WJM831T						

562	CJH122V	Bristol VRT/SL3/6LXB	Eastern Coach Works	CH41/25F	1980	Ex Thames Valley & Aldershot, 1986

601-605

Leyland Olympian ONCL10/1RZ   Northern Counties   H45/29F   1988

601	F172LBL	602	F173LBL	603	F174LBL	604	F175LBL	605	F176LBL

709	WJM817T	Leyland Leopard PSU3E/4R	Plaxton Supreme IV Express	C49F	1979	Ex Thames Valley & Aldershot, 1986
719	GGM75W	Leyland Leopard PSU3F/4R	Plaxton Supreme IV Express	C51F	1981	Ex Thames Valley & Aldershot, 1986
721	RPB951X	Leyland Leopard PSU3G/4R	Eastern Coach Works B51	C49F	1982	Ex Thames Valley & Aldershot, 1986
727	WPD30Y	Leyland Leopard PSU3G/4R	Eastern Coach Works B51	C49F	1982	Ex Thames Valley & Aldershot, 1986

740-746

Scania K113CRB   Berkhof Excellence 2000   C53F   1991

740	J740TDP	742	J742TDP	744	J744TDP	745	J745TDP	746	J746TDP
741	J741TDP	743	J743TDP						

752	YPJ203Y	Leyland Tiger TRCTL11/3R	Plaxton Paramount 3500	C50F	1983	Ex Thames Valley & Aldershot, 1986
761	A211DPB	Leyland Tiger TRCTL11/3RH	Plaxton Paramount 3200	C51F	1989	Ex Thames Valley & Aldershot, 1986

762	A212DPB	Leyland Tiger TRCTL11/3RH	Plaxton Paramount 3200	C51F	1989	Ex Thames Valley & Aldershot, 1986
765	A215DPB	Leyland Tiger TRCTL11/3RH	Plaxton Paramount 3200	C51F	1989	Ex Thames Valley & Aldershot, 1986
787	F757OJH	Volvo B10M-61	Jonckheere Jubilee P50	C53F	1989	
790	F760OJH	Volvo B10M-61	Jonckheere Jubilee P50	C53F	1989	

Special Liveries:
Railair link: 740-6.

BRIGHTON BUSES Fleet List

1-15

Leyland Atlantean AN68A/1R East Lancashire H43/31F 1978

1	TYJ1S	4	TYJ4S	7	TYJ7S	10	TYJ10S	13	TYJ13S
2	TYJ2S	5	TYJ5S	8	TYJ8S	11	TYJ11S	14	TYJ14S
3	TYJ3S	6	TYJ6S	9	TYJ9S	12	TYJ12S	15	TYJ15S

16	OAP16W	Dennis Dominator DDA134	East Lancashire	H43/31F	1981	
17	OAP17W	Dennis Dominator DDA134	East Lancashire	H43/31F	1981	
18	C718NCD	Dennis Dominator DDA1005	East Lancashire	H43/32F	1985	
19	C719NCD	Dennis Dominator DDA1005	East Lancashire	H43/32F	1985	
20	C720NCD	Dennis Dominator DDA1004	East Lancashire	DPH43/28F	1985	
21	C721NCD	Dennis Dominator DDA1004	East Lancashire	DPH43/28F	1985	
24	SPN669X	Leyland Leopard PSU3E/4R	Duple Dominant IV	C53F	1981	Ex Southend, 1988

25-31

Leyland National 2 NL116HLXB/1R B49F* 1983 *28-30 are B47F

25	XFG25Y	27	XFG27Y	29	XFG29Y	30	XFG30Y	31	XFG31Y
26	XFG26Y	28	XFG28Y						

32	LUF132F	Leyland Titan PD3/4	MCW/Cammell Laird	O39/30F	1968	
33	BCD814L	Leyland National 1151/1R/0102		B49F	1973	Ex Eastbourne, 1989
34	MCD134F	Leyland Titan PD3/4	MCW/Cammell Laird	O39/30F	1968	
35	MCD135F	Leyland Titan PD3/4	MCW/Cammell Laird	O39/30F	1968	
38	F538LUF	Leyland Lynx LX112L10ZR1R	Leyland	B47F	1989	
44	F544LUF	Leyland Lynx LX112L10ZR1R	Leyland	B47F	1989	
45	F545LUF	Leyland Lynx LX112L10ZR1R	Leyland	B47F	1989	
46	F546LUF	Leyland Lynx LX112L10ZR1R	Leyland	B47F	1989	
47	E447FWV	Leyland Lynx LX1126LXCTZR1S	Leyland	B47F	1988	
48	E448FWV	Leyland Lynx LX1126LXCTZR1S	Leyland	B47F	1988	
49	E449FWV	Leyland Lynx LX1126LXCTZR1S	Leyland	B47F	1988	

50-64

Renault-Dodge S56 Alexander AM B23F 1987-88 59/60 are DP25F

50	E450OAP	53	E453WJK	56	D456YPN	59	E459WJK	62	E462CWV
51	E451OAP	54	D454YPN	57	D457YPN	60	E460WJK	63	E463CWV
52	E452OAP	55	D455YPN	58	E458WJK	61	E461CWV	64	E464CWV

65-72

Leyland Atlantean AN68/1R East Lancashire H45/28D 1976-77 67 is H45/32F

65	OYJ65R	67	OYJ67R	69	OYJ69R	71	OYJ71R	72	OYJ72R
66	OYJ66R	68	OYJ68R	70	OYJ70R				

73	BHO440V	Leyland Leopard PSU3E/4R	Duple Dominant II	C53F	1980	Ex Southend, 1988
74	8683LJ	Dennis Javelin 11SDL1905	Duple 320	C53F	1988	
75	OJI8786	Dennis Javelin 11SDL1905	Duple 320	C53F	1988	
77	MMB977P	Leyland National 11351/1R/SC		DP48F	1975	Ex Crosville Wales, 1990
78	MMB975P	Leyland National 11351/1R/SC		DP48F	1975	Ex Crosville Wales, 1990
79	MMB973P	Leyland National 11351/1R/SC		DP48F	1975	Ex Crosville Wales, 1990
80	WOV580T	AEC Reliance 6U3ZR	Plaxton Supreme IV	C53F	1978	Ex Lewes Coach, 1988
81	PIB5144	Leyland Leopard PSU3E/4RT	Willowbrook Warrior (1991)	B48F	1980	Ex Southend, 1988
82	BTE207V	Leyland Leopard PSU3E/4RT	Duple Dominant II Express	DP51F	1980	Ex Southend, 1988
85	PIB5145	Leyland Leopard PSU3E/4RT	Willowbrook Warrior (1991)	B48F	1980	Ex Southend, 1988

92-96

Leyland Lynx LX112L10ZR1R Leyland B47F 1990

92	G992VWV	93	G993VWV	94	G994VWV	95	G995VWV	96	G996VWV

97	H909SKW	Renault S75	Whittaker-Europa	B29F	1990	
101	PTX331Y	Bedford YNT	Plaxton Supreme VI	C53F	1982	Ex Daisy, Broughton, 1985
105	WFX73X	Bedford YNT	Plaxton Supreme V	C49F	1982	Ex Marchwood, Totton, 1988

106	OJI8324	Ford R1014/S	Plaxton Supreme IV	C35F	1981	Ex Essex Coachways, London E3, 1988
107	TSV717	Bedford YNT	Plaxton Paramount 3200	C53F	1984	Ex Terminus, Crawley, 1988
108	GBO241W	Bedford YMT	Plaxton Supreme IV	C53F	1980	Ex Hills, Tredegar, 1983
109	REA946W	Bedford YMT	Plaxton Supreme IV	C53F	1980	Ex Evans, Senghenydd, 1985
110	OJI8784	Bedford YNT	Plaxton Paramount 3200	C53F	1984	Ex Lyford, Holcombe, 1990
111	OJI8785	Bedford YNT	Plaxton Paramount 3200	C53F	1984	Ex Pathfinder, Chadwell Heath, 1990
120	H920BPN	Van Hool T815H	Van Hool Alizée HE	C49FT	1991	
121	H921BPN	Van Hool T815H	Van Hool Alizée HE	C49FT	1991	
122	H922BPN	Mercedes-Benz 709D	Made-to-Measure	C24F	1991	

Previous Registrations:

8683LJ	E474FWV	OJI8784	A103MAC	PIB5144	UTD203T
H922BPN	H552EVM	OJI8785	A840PPP	PIB5145	UTD204T
OJI8324	NMC66X	OJI8786	E475FWV	TSV717	B272HCD

Special Liveries:

Campings: 101-111
Overall Advertisements: 17-9, 27, 79, 94

BRIGHTON & HOVE Fleet List

55-80

Leyland National 11351A/2R — B44D — 1977-78 Ex Southdown, 1986

55	UFG55S	59	UFG59S	66	WYJ166S	79	YCD79T	80	YCD80T
57	UFG57S	63	WYJ163S	67	WYJ167S				

106	AYJ106T	Leyland National 11351A/1R		B52F	1979	Ex Southdown, 1986
110	C110UBC	Scania N112DR	East Lancashire	H46/33F	1986	Ex Leicester, 1989
111	C111UBC	Scania N112DR	East Lancashire	H46/33F	1986	Ex Leicester, 1989
112	C112UBC	Scania N112DR	East Lancashire	H46/33F	1986	Ex Leicester, 1989
113	C113UBC	Scania N112DR	East Lancashire	H46/33F	1986	Ex Leicester, 1989
127	JWV127W	Leyland National 2 NL116L11/1R		B52F	1980	Ex Southdown, 1986
128	JWV128W	Leyland National 2 NL116L11/1R		B52F	1980	Ex Southdown, 1986

150-157

Leyland National 2 NL116HLXCT/1R — B49F — 1985 Ex Southdown, 1986

150	C450OAP	152	C452OAP	154	C454OAP	156	C456OAP	157	C457OAP
151	C451OAP	153	C453OAP	155	C455OAP				

205	C205PCD	Mercedes-Benz L608D	Alexander AM	B20F	1985	Ex Southdown, 1986
206	C206PCD	Mercedes-Benz L608D	Alexander AM	B20F	1985	Ex Southdown, 1986
210	C210PCD	Mercedes-Benz L608D	Alexander AM	B20F	1985	Ex Southdown, 1986

250-265

Bristol VRT/SL3/6LXB — Eastern Coach Works — H43/31F — 1980-81 Ex Southdown, 1986

250	JWV250W	259	JWV259W	261	JWV261W	263	JWV263W	265	JWV265W
257	JWV257W	260	JWV260W	262	JWV262W	264	JWV264W		

270	JWV270W	Bristol VRT/SL3/680	Eastern Coach Works	H43/31F	1981	Ex Southdown, 1986
272	JWV272W	Bristol VRT/SL3/680	Eastern Coach Works	H43/31F	1981	Ex Southdown, 1986
273	JWV273W	Bristol VRT/SL3/680	Eastern Coach Works	H43/31F	1981	Ex Southdown, 1986
277	VVV964W	Bristol VRT/SL3/6LXB	Eastern Coach Works	H43/31F	1981	Ex Milton Keynes City Bus, 1986
278	VVV958W	Bristol VRT/SL3/6LXB	Eastern Coach Works	H43/31F	1981	Ex Milton Keynes City Bus, 1986
279	VVV959W	Bristol VRT/SL3/6LXB	Eastern Coach Works	H43/31F	1981	Ex Milton Keynes City Bus, 1986

340-359

Mercedes-Benz 811D — Wadham Stringer — B31F* — 1989 Ex Bournemouth, 1990
*359 is DP31F

340	F40XPR	344	F44XPR	348	F48XPR	352	G52BEL	356	G56BEL
341	F41XPR	345	F45XPR	349	F49XPR	353	G53BEL	357	G57BEL
342	F42XPR	346	F46XPR	350	G50BEL	354	G54BEL	359	G59BEL
343	F43XPR	347	F47XPR	351	G51BEL	355	G55BEL		

406	C376PCD	Leyland Tiger TRCTL11/3RH	Plaxton Paramount 3500 II	C49FT	1986	
407	C377PCD	Leyland Tiger TRCTL11/3RH	Plaxton Paramount 3500 II	C49FT	1986	
408	C378PCD	Leyland Tiger TRCTL11/3RH	Plaxton Paramount 3500 II	C49FT	1986	
409	C379PCD	Leyland Tiger TRCTL11/3RH	Plaxton Paramount 3500 II	C51F	1986	
501	E501EFG	Dennis Javelin 12SDA1913	Duple 320	C53FT	1988	
502	E502EFG	Dennis Javelin 12SDA1913	Duple 320	C53FT	1988	

503	E503EFG	Dennis Javelin 12SDA1913	Duple 320	C53FT	1988	
504	F504LAP	Dennis Javelin 12SDA1913	Plaxton Paramount 3200 III	C53FT	1989	
505	F505LAP	Dennis Javelin 12SDA1913	Plaxton Paramount 3200 III	C53FT	1989	
506	F506LAP	Dennis Javelin 12SDA1913	Plaxton Paramount 3200 III	C53FT	1989	
507	G507SAP	Dennis Javelin 12SDA1928	Duple 320	C53FT	1990	
508	G508SAP	Dennis Javelin 12SDA1928	Duple 320	C53FT	1990	
509	G509SAP	Dennis Javelin 12SDA1928	Duple 320	C53FT	1990	
584	SNJ684R	Bristol VRT/SL3/6LXB	Eastern Coach Works	H43/31F	1977	Ex Southdown, 1986
590	SNJ590R	Bristol VRT/SL3/6LXB	Eastern Coach Works	H43/31F	1977	Ex Southdown, 1986
592	SNJ592R	Bristol VRT/SL3/6LXB	Eastern Coach Works	H43/31F	1977	Ex Southdown, 1986
593	SNJ593R	Bristol VRT/SL3/6LXB	Eastern Coach Works	H43/31F	1977	Ex Southdown, 1986

594-603

Bristol VRT/SL3/6LXB   Eastern Coach Works   CO43/27D   1977   Ex Southdown, 1986

| 594 | TNJ994S | 598 | TNJ998S | 600 | TPN100S | 602 | TPN102S | 603 | TPN103S |
| 595 | TNJ995S | 599 | TNJ999S | 601 | TPN101S | | | | |

606	UWV606S	Bristol VRT/SL3/6LXB	Eastern Coach Works	CO43/31F	1977	Ex Southdown, 1986
615	UWV615S	Bristol VRT/SL3/6LXB	Eastern Coach Works	CO43/31F	1978	Ex Southdown, 1986
619	UWV619S	Bristol VRT/SL3/6LXB	Eastern Coach Works	CO43/31F	1978	Ex Southdown, 1986

624-633

Bristol VRT/SL3/6LXB   Eastern Coach Works   H43/27D   1977   Ex Southdown, 1986 *624 is H43/27F

| 624 | UFG624S | 626 | UFG626S | 628 | UFG628S | 630 | UFG630S | 632 | UFG632S |
| 625 | UFG625S | 627 | UFG627S | 629 | UFG629S | 631 | UFG631S | 633 | UFG633S |

635-651

Bristol VRT/SL3/6LXB   Eastern Coach Works   H43/31F   1978   Ex Southdown, 1986

| 635 | XAP635S | 639 | XAP639S | 641 | XAP641S | 645 | XAP645S | 650 | AAP650T |
| 638 | XAP638S | 640 | XAP640S | 642 | XAP642S | 646 | AAP646T | 651 | AAP651T |

653-667

Bristol VRT/SL3/6LXB   Eastern Coach Works   H43/27D   1978-79 Ex Southdown, 1986

653	AAP653T	656	AAP656T	659	AAP659T	664	AAP664T	666	AAP666T
654	AAP654T	657	AAP657T	663	AAP663T	665	AAP665T	667	AAP667T
655	AAP655T	658	AAP658T						

674-699

Bristol VRT/SL3/6LXB   Eastern Coach Works   H43/31F   1979-80 Ex Southdown, 1986

| 674 | EAP974V | 676 | EAP976V | 689 | EAP989V | 694 | EAP994V | 698 | EAP998V |
| 675 | EAP975V | 679 | EAP979V | 693 | EAP993V | 695 | EAP995V | 699 | EAP999V |

701-710

Scania N112DRB   East Lancashire   H47/33F   1988

| 701 | E701EFG | 703 | E703EFG | 705 | E705EFG | 707 | E707EFG | 709 | E709EFG |
| 702 | E702EFG | 704 | E704EFG | 706 | E706EFG | 708 | E708EFG | 710 | E710EFG |

711-730

Scania N113DRB   East Lancashire   H47/33F   1989-90

711	F711LFG	715	F715LFG	719	F719LFG	723	G723RYJ	727	G727RYJ
712	F712LFG	716	F716LFG	720	F720LFG	724	G724RYJ	728	G728RYJ
713	F713LFG	717	F717LFG	721	G721RYJ	725	G725RYJ	729	G729RYJ
714	F714LFG	718	F718LFG	722	G722RYJ	726	G726RYJ	730	G730RYJ

| 6447 | HAP985 | Bristol KSW6G | Eastern Coach Works | H32/28R | 1953 | Ex preservation, 1986 |

Special Liveries:

Centrebus: 205/6/10
Shearings Holidays: 501-3/6/8/9.
Traditional BH&D livery: 6447

EASTBOURNE BUSES Fleet List

3	C530KNO	Volvo B10M-61	Plaxton Paramount 3500 II	C53F	1985	Ex Essex Police, 1991
4	E804DPN	Volvo B10M-61	Plaxton Paramount 3500 III	C53F	1988	
5	E805DPN	Volvo B10M-61	Plaxton Paramount 3500 III	C53F	1988	
6	C347SGD	Volvo B10M-61	Caetano Algarve	C53F	1986	Ex Park, Hamilton, 1989
7	H908DTP	Dennis Dart 9SDL3002	Wadham Stringer Portsdown	B35F	1991	Ex Wadham Stringer demonstrator
8	H840GDY	Dennis Dart 9SDL3002	Wadham Stringer Portsdown	B35F	1990	
9	H841GDY	Dennis Dart 9SDL3002	Wadham Stringer Portsdown	B35F	1990	

10	G114FJK	Dennis Javelin 11SDL1914	Duple 300	B55F	1990	
11	G911RPN	Dennis Javelin 11SDL1914	Duple 300	B55F	1989	
12	UPB200S	Leyland National 10351A/1R		DP39F	1976	Ex London Country NW, 1990
16	SPC270R	Leyland National 10351A/1R		B41F	1977	Ex London Country NW, 1989
21	J221FUF	Dennis Dart 9.8SDL3012	Wadham Stringer Portsdown	B43F	1991	
22	J122FUF	Dennis Dart 9.8SDL3004	Wadham Stringer Portsdown	B43F	1992	
23	J223FUF	Dennis Javelin 11SDL1924	Wadham Stringer Vanguard II	B55F	1992	
24	J124FUF	Dennis Javelin 11SDL1924	Wadham Stringer Vanguard II	B55F	1991	
25	G25HDW	Dennis Javelin 11SDL1907	Duple 300	B55F	1990	Ex Bebb, Llantwit Fardre, 1991
26	G28HDW	Dennis Javelin 11SDL1907	Duple 300	B55F	1990	Ex Bebb, Llantwit Fardre, 1991
27	J127LHC	Dennis Javelin 11SDL1924	Plaxton Derwent	DP53F	1991	
28	JJG3P	Leyland Atlantean AN68/1R	Eastern Coach Works	H43/31F	1976	Ex East Kent, 1991
29	NNO62P	Leyland Atlantean AN68A/1R	Eastern Coach Works	H43/31F	1975	Ex Colchester, 1991
30	NNO64P	Leyland Atlantean AN68A/1R	Eastern Coach Works	H43/31F	1975	Ex Colchester, 1991
32	JJG2P	Leyland Atlantean AN68/1R	Eastern Coach Works	H43/31F	1976	Ex East Kent, 1990
33	JJG6P	Leyland Atlantean AN68/1R	Eastern Coach Works	H43/31F	1976	Ex East Kent, 1990
34	YJK934V	Leyland Atlantean AN68A/2R	East Lancashire	H47/35F	1979	
35	YJK935V	Leyland Atlantean AN68A/2R	East Lancashire	H47/35F	1979	
38	MPN138W	Dennis Dominator DD120	East Lancashire	H43/31F	1981	
39	MPN139W	Dennis Dominator DD120	East Lancashire	H43/31F	1981	
40	MPN140W	Dennis Dominator DD122	East Lancashire	H47/35F	1981	
41	MPN141W	Dennis Dominator DD122	East Lancashire	H47/35F	1981	

42-46

		Dennis Dominator DDA154	East Lancashire	H43/31F	1982

42	FDY142X	43	FDY143X	44	FDY144X	45	FDY145X	46	FDY146X

47-58

		Leyland Olympian ONCL10/2RZ	Northern Counties	H47/30F	1988

47	E847DPN	50	E850DPN	53	E853DPN	55	E855DPN	57	E857DPN
48	E848DPN	51	E851DPN	54	E854DPN	56	E856DPN	58	E858DPN
49	E849DPN	52	E852DPN						

59	JSL280X	Dennis Dominator DDA139	East Lancashire	H50/33F	1981	Ex Brighton, 1990
65	LDX75G	Leyland Atlantean PDR1/1	Eastern Coach Works	O43/31F	1968	Ex Ipswich, 1980
66	LDX76G	Leyland Atlantean PDR1/1	Eastern Coach Works	O43/31F	1968	Ex Ipswich, 1980
81	LFR532F	Leyland Titan PD3/11	MCW	H41/30R	1968	Ex Blackpool, 1989
82	DHC782E	Leyland Titan PD2A/30	East Lancashire	H32/28R	1967	

Named vehicles:
65 *Eastbourne Queen*, 66 *Eastbourne King*.

Special Liveries:
Overall Advertisements: 21, 42, 54.

EAST KENT Fleet List

1	C701FKE	Ford Transit 190L	Dormobile	B16F	1986
4	C704FKE	Ford Transit 190L	Dormobile	B16F	1986
12	C712FKE	Ford Transit 190L	Dormobile	B16F	1986

28-42

		Freight Rover Sherpa 365	Dormobile	B16F	1986

28	C728FKE	35	C735FKE	36	C736HKK	41	C741HKK	42	C742HKK

43	D743LKE	Freight Rover Sherpa 374	Dormobile	B16F	1986
44	D744LKE	Freight Rover Sherpa 374	Dormobile	B16F	1986
46	G446VKK	Iveco Daily 49.10	Carlyle Dailybus	B23F	1990
47	G447VKK	Iveco Daily 49.10	Carlyle Dailybus	B23F	1990

51-70

		Iveco Daily 49.10	Robin Hood	B23F	1987

51	E151UKR	55	E155UKR	59	E159UKR	63	E163UKR	67	E167UKR
52	E152UKR	56	E156UKR	60	E160UKR	64	E164UKR	68	E168UKR
53	E153UKR	57	E157UKR	61	E161UKR	65	E165UKR	69	E169UKR
54	E154UKR	58	E158UKR	62	E162UKR	66	E166UKR	70	E170UKR

71-75

		Iveco Daily 49.10	Robin Hood	B23F	1989

71	F71FKK	72	F72FKK	73	F73FKK	74	F74FKK	75	F75FKK

80-87

							Iveco Daily 49.10		Robin Hood	B19F	1987	
80	E580TKJ	82	E582TKJ	84	E584TKJ	86	E586TKJ		87	E587TKJ		
81	E581TKJ	83	E583TKJ	85	E585TKJ							

91	G491RKK	Iveco Daily 49.10	Carlyle Dailybus	B23F	1990
92	G492RKK	Iveco Daily 49.10	Carlyle Dailybus	B23F	1990
93	G493RKK	Iveco Daily 49.10	Carlyle Dailybus	B23F	1990
94	G494RKK	Iveco Daily 49.10	Carlyle Dailybus	B23F	1990

95-104

Iveco Daily 49.10   Phoenix   B23F   1990-91

95	G95SKR	97	G97SKR	101	H101EKR	103	H103EKR	104	H104EKR
96	G96SKR	98	G98SKR	102	H102EKR				

112	J112LKO	Iveco Daily 49.10	Carlyle Dailybus	B23F	1991
113	J113LKO	Iveco Daily 49.10	Carlyle Dailybus	B23F	1991
114	J114LKO	Iveco Daily 49.10	Carlyle Dailybus	B23F	1991

115-121

Iveco Daily 49.10   Dormobile Routemaker   B23F   1991

115	J115LKO	117	J117LKO	119	J119LKO	120	J120LKO	121	J121LKO
116	J116LKO	118	J118LKO						

226	D226VCD	Iveco Daily 49.10	Robin Hood	B21F	1986	Ex Brighton & Hove, 1990
230	D230VCD	Iveco Daily 49.10	Robin Hood	B21F	1986	Ex Brighton & Hove, 1990
231	D231VCD	Iveco Daily 49.10	Robin Hood	B21F	1986	Ex Brighton & Hove, 1990
664	C664BEX	Freight Rover Sherpa 365	Dormobile	B16F	1986	Ex Eastern Counties, 1989
668	D668HAH	Freight Rover Sherpa 374	Dormobile	B16F	1986	Ex Eastern Counties, 1989
1024	PNH24N	Leyland National 11351/2R		B30D	1974	Ex Robson, Thornaby, 1991
1027	PNH27N	Leyland National 11351/2R		B30D	1974	Ex Robson, Thornaby, 1991
1060	NPD160L	Leyland National 1151/1R/0402		B30D	1973	Ex London Country, 1984
1067	NPD167L	Leyland National 1151/1R/0402		B30D	1973	Ex London Country, 1984

1081-1089

Leyland National 11351A/1R   DP48F   1977

1081	NFN81R	1083	NFN83R	1086	NFN86R	1088	NFN88R	1089	NFN89R
1082	NFN82R	1084	NFN84R	1087	NFN87R				

1115	MFN115R	Leyland National 11351A/1R		B49F	1976
1117	MFN117R	Leyland National 11351A/1R		B49F	1976
1118	MFN118R	Leyland National 11351A/1R		B49F	1976
1145	NPD145L	Leyland National 1151/1R/0402		B30D	1973	Ex London Country, 1984
1153	NPD153L	Leyland National 1151/1R/0402		B30D	1973	Ex London Country, 1984
1156	NPD156L	Leyland National 1151/1R/0402		B30D	1973	Ex London Country, 1984
1159	NPD159L	Leyland National 1151/1R/0402		B30D	1973	Ex London Country, 1984
1255	Q255GRW	Leyland National 2 NL116AL11/2R		B30D	1981	Ex Dunlop, Coventry, 1988
1300	GAE300N	Leyland National 11351/2R		B30D	1974	Ex City Line, Bristol, 1988
1344	PJJ344S	Leyland National 10351A/1R		B41F	1977	
1345	PJJ345S	Leyland National 10351A/1R		B41F	1977	
1346	PJJ346S	Leyland National 10351A/1R		B41F	1977	
1401	J401LKO	DAF SB220LC550	Optare Delta	B49F	1991	
1402	J402LKO	DAF SB220LC550	Optare Delta	B49F	1991	
1403	J403LKO	DAF SB220LC550	Optare Delta	B49F	1991	
1546	GFN546N	Leyland National 10351/1R		B40F	1975	
1552	GFN552N	Leyland National 10351/1R		B37F	1975	
1559	NOE559R	Leyland National 11351A/1R		B30D	1976	Ex City Line, Bristol, 1988
1851	LFB851P	Leyland National 11351A/2R		B30D	1976	Ex City Line, Bristol, 1988

1890-1900

Leyland National 11351A/1R   B49F   1976

1890	JJG890P	1893	JJG893P	1895	JJG895P	1898	JJG898P	1900	JJG900P
1892	JJG892P								

7016-7024

Bristol VRT/SL3/6LXB   Willowbrook   H43/31F   1977-78

7016	PJJ16S	7021	PJJ21S	7022	PJJ22S	7023	PJJ23S	7024	PJJ24S

7041-7046

Bristol VRT/SL3/6LXB   Eastern Coach Works   H43/31F   1976

7041	MFN41R	7042	MFN42R	7043	MFN43R	7045	MFN45R	7046	MFN46R

7613	UWV613S	Bristol VRT/SL3/6LXB	Eastern Coach Works	CO43/31F	1977	Ex Southdown, 1991			
7616	UWV616S	Bristol VRT/SL3/6LXB	Eastern Coach Works	CO43/31F	1978	Ex Southdown, 1991			
7622	UWV622S	Bristol VRT/SL3/6LXB	Eastern Coach Works	CO43/31F	1978	Ex Southdown, 1991			

7650-7685

Bristol VRT/SL3/6LXB · Eastern Coach Works · H43/31F · 1980-81 · 7655 rebodied 1983

7650	XJJ650V	7658	XJJ658V	7665	XJJ665V	7672	BJG672V	7679	CJJ679W
7651	XJJ651V	7659	XJJ659V	7666	XJJ666V	7673	BJG673V	7680	SKL680X
7652	XJJ652V	7660	XJJ660V	7667	XJJ667V	7674	BJG674V	7681	SKL681X
7653	XJJ653V	7661	XJJ661V	7668	XJJ668V	7675	BJG675V	7682	SKL682X
7654	XJJ654V	7662	XJJ662V	7669	XJJ669V	7676	CJJ676W	7683	SKL683X
7655	XJJ655V	7663	XJJ663V	7670	XJJ670V	7677	CJJ677W	7684	SKL684X
7657	XJJ657V	7664	XJJ664V	7671	BJG671V	7678	CJJ678W	7685	SKL685X

7746-7755

MCW Metrobus Mk2 DR132/11 · MCW · H46/31F · 1988

7746	E746SKR	7748	E748SKR	7750	E750SKR	7752	E752SKR	7754	E754UKR
7747	E747SKR	7749	E749SKR	7751	E751SKR	7753	E753SKR	7755	E755UKR

7761-7767

MCW Metrobus Mk2 DR132/15 · MCW · DPH43/27F · 1989

7761	F761EKM	7763	F763EKM	7765	F765EKM	7766	F766EKM	7767	F767EKM
7762	F762EKM	7764	F764EKM						

7771-7775

MCW Metrobus Mk2 DR132/14 · MCW · H46/31F · 1989

7771	F771EKM	7772	F772EKM	7773	F773EKM	7774	F774EKM	7775	F775EKM

7781	F781KKP	Scania N113DRB	Alexander RH	H47/33F	1989
7782	F782KKP	Scania N113DRB	Alexander RH	H47/33F	1989

7801-7810

Leyland Olympian ON2R56C16Z4 · Northern Counties · H51/34F · 1990

7801	H801BKK	7803	H803BKK	7805	H805BKK	7807	H807BKK	7809	H809BKK
7802	H802BKK	7804	H804BKK	7806	H806BKK	7808	H808BKK	7810	H810BKK

7811	J811NKK	Leyland Olympian ON2R50C13Z4	Northern Counties	H47/30F	1992
7812	J812NKK	Leyland Olympian ON2R50C13Z4	Northern Counties	H47/30F	1992
7813	J813NKK	Leyland Olympian ON2R50C13Z4	Northern Counties	H47/30F	1992
7814	J814NKK	Leyland Olympian ON2R50C13Z4	Northern Counties	H47/30F	1992

7973-7991

Bristol VRT/SL3/6LXB · Willowbrook · H43/31F · 1978

7973	RVB973S	7976	RVB976S	7982	TFN982T	7987	TFN987T	7990	TFN990T
7974	RVB974S	7978	RVB978S	7985	TFN985T	7988	TFN988T	7991	TFN991T
7975	RVB975S	7979	RVB979S	7986	TFN986T	7989	TFN989T		

8192	XSU912	MCW Metroliner HR131/2	MCW	C49FT	1984	Ex Premier Travel, 1988
8211	D211VEV	Scania K112CRB	Berkhof Esprite 350	C41FT	1987	On loan to East Kent
8244	LDZ3144	MCW Metroliner HR131/6	MCW	C49FT	1985	Ex Premier Travel, 1988
8245	LDZ3145	MCW Metroliner HR131/6	MCW	C49FT	1985	Ex Premier Travel, 1988
8246	XYK976	MCW Metroliner HR131/6	MCW	C49FT	1985	Ex Premier Travel, 1988
8399	XDU599	MCW Metroliner HR131/1	MCW	C49FT	1983	Ex MCW, Birmingham, 1988
8513	XSU913	Bova FHD12-280	Bova Futura	C49FT	1984	Ex Marinair, 1991

8828-8837

Leyland Leopard PSU3G/4R · Eastern Coach Works B51 · DP47F* · 1982 · *8828 is DP47F, 8837 is DP49F

8828	UKE828X	8832	BKR832Y	8835	BKR835Y	8836	BKR836Y	8837	BKR837Y
8831	UKE831X	8834	BKR834Y						

8838-8842

Leyland Tiger TRCTL11/3R · Plaxton Paramount 3200 E · C53F · 1983

8838	TSU638	8839	TSU639	8840	TSU640	8841	TSU641	8842	TSU642

8843	6540FN	MCW Metroliner CR126/1	MCW	C51F	1983
8844	PFN873	MCW Metroliner CR126/2	MCW	C51F	1983
8846	572RKJ	MCW Metroliner CR126/2	MCW	C51F	1983
8847	ESU247	MCW Metroliner CR126/2	MCW	C51F	1983

8848-8853

MCW Metroliner CR126/8 · MCW · C51F · 1984

8848	WSU448	8850	WSU450	8851	WSU451	8852	WSU452	8853	WSU453
8849	XMW285								

8854	E854UKR	MCW Metroliner HR131/12	MCW	C51F	1988
8855	E855UKR	MCW Metroliner HR131/12	MCW	C51F	1988
8856	J856NKK	Scania K93CRB	Plaxton Paramount 3500 III	C49FT	1992

8901-8908 Volvo B10M-60 Plaxton Expressliner C49FT 1989

| 8901 | G901PKK | 8903 | G903PKK | 8905 | G905PKK | 8907 | G907PKK | 8908 | G908PKK |
| 8902 | G902PKK | 8904 | G904PKK | 8906 | G906PKK | | | | |

| ~~8909~~ | ~~J909NKP~~ | Volvo B10M-60 | Plaxton Expressliner | C46FT | 1992 | |
| 8996 | C996FKM | Bova FHD12-280 | Bova Futura | C49FT | 1986 | Ex Marinair, 1991 |

Previous Registrations:

572RKJ	FKK846Y	TSU639	FKK839Y	WSU452	B852TKL
6540FN	FKK843Y	TSU640	FKK840Y	WSU453	B853TKL
ESU247	FKK847Y	TSU641	FKK841Y	XDU599	A543WOB, ABM399A
LDZ3144	B244JVA	TSU642	FKK842Y	XMW285	A849OKK
LDZ3145	B245JVA	WSU448	A848OKK	XSU912	B192JVA
PFN873	FKK844Y	WSU450	B850TKL	XSU913	A513HBC
TSU638	FKK838Y	WSU451	B851TKL	XYK976	B246JVA

Special Liveries:

Canterbury Park & Ride:	1401-3
Freedom coach:	8211
Hoverspeed:	1027, 1255, 1559, 1851.
National Express:	8513, 8901-9, 8996.
Overall Advertisements:	51/5/6, 68, 71, 86, 101-4/13/20/1, 230, 1546, 7661/74/82/84, 7748, 7988, 8831
Sainsbury's/Co-op:	83, 1893, 1900
SeaCat:	1552.
Sealink:	1060/7, 1145/53/6/9.

Named vehicles:
7805 *Odyssey*, 7807 *Enterprise*, 7808 *Sir Thomas More*, 7809 *Pegasus*, 7810 *Thomas Becket*

GREY-GREEN Non-LT Fleet List

Note: The LT fleet of Grey-Green may be found in London Bus Handbook, Part 2

101	B101XYH	Auwaerter Neoplan N122/3	Plaxton Paramount 4000	CH55/20DT	1984	
102	B102XYH	Auwaerter Neoplan N122/3	Plaxton Paramount 4000	CH55/20DT	1985	
103	C103CYE	Scania K112TRS	Plaxton Paramount 4000 II	CH57/18CT	1985	
107	E107JYV	Scania K92CRB	East Lancashire	DPH45/30F	1987	
108	E108JYV	Scania K92CRB	East Lancashire	DPH45/30F	1988	
472	DTG372V	MCW Metrobus DR102/15	MCW	H46/32F	1980	Ex Newport, 1992

492-498 Daimler Fleetline CRG6LXB Northern Counties H43/32F 1974-75 Ex Greater Manchester, 1987

| 492 | GND492N | 493 | GND493N | 496 | GDB162N | 497 | GDB163N | 498 | GDB164N |

801	D101NDW	Leyland Lynx LX112TL11ZR1R	Leyland	B51F	1987	Ex Merthyr Tydfil, 1989
802	D102NDW	Leyland Lynx LX112TL11ZR1R	Leyland	B51F	1987	Ex Merthyr Tydfil, 1989
803	D108NDW	Leyland Lynx LX112TL11ZR1R	Leyland	B51F	1987	Ex Merthyr Tydfil, 1989
804	LPB203P	Leyland National 10351/1R		B41F	1976	Ex County, 1992
805	LPB211P	Leyland National 10351/1R		B41F	1976	Ex County, 1992
806	NPK229R	Leyland National 10351A/1R		B41F	1976	Ex County, 1992
807	SPC265R	Leyland National 10351A/1R		B41F	1977	Ex County, 1992
808	UPB296S	Leyland National 10351A/1R		B41F	1977	Ex County, 1992
874	C874CYX	Volvo B10M-61	Plaxton Paramount 3200 II	C53F	1986	
875	C875CYX	Volvo B10M-61	Plaxton Paramount 3200 II	C53F	1986	
876	C876CYX	Volvo B10M-61	Plaxton Paramount 3200 II	C53F	1986	
877	C877CYX	Volvo B10M-61	Plaxton Paramount 3200 II	C53F	1986	
878	D878FYL	Volvo B10M-61	Duple 320	C53F	1987	
879	D879FYL	Volvo B10M-61	Plaxton Paramount 3200 III	C53F	1987	
880	D880FYL	Volvo B10M-61	Plaxton Paramount 3200 III	C53F	1987	
881	D881FYL	Volvo B10M-61	Plaxton Paramount 3200 III	C53F	1987	
882	D882FYL	Volvo B10M-61	Plaxton Paramount 3500 III	C49FT	1987	

883	D883FYL	Volvo B10M-61	Plaxton Paramount 3500 III	C49FT	1987	
884	D884FYL	Volvo B10M-61	Plaxton Paramount 3500 III	C49FT	1987	
891	E891KYW	Volvo B10M-61	Duple 320	C53F	1988	
892	E892KYW	Volvo B10M-61	Duple 320	C53F	1988	
893	E893KYW	Volvo B10M-61	Duple 320	C53F	1988	
894	E894KYW	Volvo B10M-61	Duple 320	C53F	1988	
895	E895KYW	Scania K92CRB	Van Hool Alizée	C53F	1988	
896	E896KYW	Scania K92CRB	Van Hool Alizée	C53F	1988	
897	E897KYW	Scania K92CRB	Van Hool Alizée	C53F	1988	
898	E898KYW	Scania K92CRB	Van Hool Alizée	C53F	1988	

899-904

		Volvo B10M-61		Van Hool Alizée		C49FT	1988	*899/900 are C53F
899	E899KYW	**901**	E901MUC	**902**	E902MUC	**903**	E903MUC	**904**	E904MUC
900	E900KYW							

905-910

		DAF MB230LB		Van Hool Alizée		C49FT	1990	
905	G905TYR	**907**	G907TYR	**908**	G908TYR	**909**	G909TYR	**910**	G910TYR
906	G906TYR							

Special Liveries:
Eurolines: 903-8

THE KINGS FERRY Fleet List

0.1	PRX207B	Leyland Titan PD3/4	Northern Counties	F039/30F	1964	Ex Southdown, 1988
0.2	FNM736Y	Mercedes-Benz L508D	Reeve Burgess	C19F	1983	Ex Smith, Challock, 1991
0.3	327WTF	Bedford VAS5	Plaxton Supreme	C29F	1979	Acquired, 1988
0.4	HEW311Y	Mercedes-Benz L608D	Reeve Burgess	C16F	1983	Ex The Bee Line, 1991
0.7	GIL8593	Mercedes-Benz L307D	Devon Conversions	C12F	1983	Ex Jones, Market Drayton, 1991
2.1	H9KFC	Toyota HDB30R	Caetano Optimo II	C21F	1991	
2.2	H10KFC	Toyota HDB30R	Caetano Optimo II	C21F	1991	
3.1	H7KFC	MAN 10-180	Berkhof Excellence 1000	C33F	1990	
3.2	H8KFC	MAN 10-180	Berkhof Excellence 1000	C33F	1991	
4.1	GIL8490	Mercedes-Benz 0303/15R	Mercedes-Benz	C49FT	1988	Ex Scarlet Band, W Cornforth, 1991

4.2-4.6

		Mercedes-Benz 0303/2	Mercedes-Benz	C49FT	1991	
4.2	H2KFC	**4.3**	H3KFC	**4.4**	H4KFC	**4.5**	H5KFC	**4.6**	H6KFC

4.7	MIB552	DAF MB230LB615	Caetano Algarve	C49FT	1988	Ex Chartercoach, Gt Oakley, 1990
4.15	GIL2786	Bova FHD12-290	Bova Futura	C51FT	1990	
4.16	GIL2784	Bova FHD12-290	Bova Futura	C51FT	1989	
4.17	GIL2785	Bova FHD12-290	Bova Futura	C51FT	1989	
4.19	G997RKN	Volvo B10M-60	Caetano Algarve	C49FT	1990	
4.20	G998RKN	Volvo B10M-60	Caetano Algarve	C49FT	1990	
4.21	G999RKN	Volvo B10M-60	Caetano Algarve	C49FT	1990	
4.22	G961UKL	Bova FHD12-290	Bova Futura	C51FT	1990	
4.23	G994UKL	Bova FHD12-290	Bova Futura	C51FT	1990	
4.24	H17KFC	Mercedes-Benz 0303	Plaxton Paramount 3500 III	C49FT	1991	
4.25	H18KFC	Mercedes-Benz 0303	Plaxton Paramount 3500 III	C49FT	1991	
4.26	J3KFC	Scania K113CRB	Berkhof Excellence 2000	C49FT	1992	
4.27	J4KFC	Scania K113CRB	Berkhof Excellence 2000	C49FT	1992	
4.28	J5KFC	Scania K113CRB	Berkhof Excellence 2000	C49FT	1992	
4.29	J6KFC	Scania K113CRB	Berkhof Excellence 2000	C49FT	1992	

5.1-5.5

		Volvo B10M-60	Caetano Algarve	C53F	1989	
5.1	G997OKK	**5.2**	G998OKK	**5.3**	G545NKJ	**5.4**	G546NKJ	**5.5**	G996OKK

5.6	H14KFC	Mercedes-Benz 0303	Plaxton Paramount 3500 III	C53F	1991	
5.7	H16KFC	Mercedes-Benz 0303	Plaxton Paramount 3500 III	C53F	1991	
5.8	H19KFC	Mercedes-Benz 0303	Plaxton Paramount 3500 III	C53F	1991	
5.9	G991OKK	DAF MB230LB615	Caetano Algarve	C53F	1989	
5.10	G999OKK	DAF MB230LB615	Caetano Algarve	C53F	1989	
5.11	H20KFC	Mercedes-Benz 0303	Plaxton Paramount 3500 III	C53F	1991	
5.12	J20KFC	Dennis Javelin 12SDA2106	Berkhof Excellence 1000	C57F	1991	
5.13	J19KFC	Dennis Javelin 12SDA2106	Berkhof Excellence 1000	C57F	1992	

6.1	PIA892	Volvo B10M-53	Berkhof Emperor 395	CH51/11DT 1984	
7.4	GIL4876	Auwaerter Neoplan N122/3	Auwaerter Skyliner	CH57/20CT 1986	Ex Tayside Travel, 1990
7.5	MIB657	Auwaerter Neoplan N122/3	Auwaerter Skyliner	CH57/20CT 1985	Ex Shaw, Bedworth, 1989

Previous Registrations:

327WTF	HRO446V	GIL8490	E989KJF	MIB657	1KOV, B662GWF
GIL2784	F680JKR	GIL8593	NMA711Y	PIA892	B570YJN
GIL2785	F999JKR	MIB552	E179KNH	PRX207B	410DCD
GIL4876	C725JTL				

MAIDSTONE & DISTRICT Fleet List

C175	TSU646	Leyland Tiger TRCTL11/3R	Plaxton Paramount 3200 E	C53F	1983	
C186	E186XKO	Leyland Tiger TRCTL11/3ARH	Plaxton Paramount 3500 III	C53F	1988	
C187	E187XKO	Leyland Tiger TRCTL11/3ARH	Plaxton Paramount 3500 III	C53F	1988	
C188	F188HKK	Leyland Tiger TRCTL10/3RZA	Duple 340	C53F	1989	
C189	F189HKK	Leyland Tiger TRCTL10/3RZA	Duple 340	C53F	1989	
1000	C203PCD	Mercedes-Benz L608D	Alexander AM	B20F	1986	Ex Brighton & Hove, 1990

1001-1039

	Mercedes-Benz L608D		Rootes	B20F	1986

1001	C201EKJ	1009	C209EKJ	1017	C217EKJ	1025	D25KKP	1033	D33KKP
1002	C202EKJ	1010	C210EKJ	1018	C218EKJ	1026	D26KKP	1034	D34KKP
1003	C203EKJ	1011	C211EKJ	1019	C219EKJ	1027	D27KKP	1035	D35KKP
1004	C204EKJ	1012	C212EKJ	1020	C220EKJ	1028	D28KKP	1036	D36KKP
1005	C205EKJ	1013	C213EKJ	1021	C221EKJ	1029	D29KKP	1037	D37KKP
1006	C206EKJ	1014	C214EKJ	1022	D22KKP	1030	D30KKP	1038	D38KKP
1007	C207EKJ	1015	C215EKJ	1023	D23KKP	1031	D31KKP	1039	D39KKP
1008	C208EKJ	1016	C216EKJ	1024	D24KKP	1032	D32KKP		

1040	D441RKE	Mercedes-Benz 609D	Reeve Burgess	B20F	1987	Ex Marinair, Canterbury, 1988

1041-1087

	Mercedes-Benz 609D		Reeve Burgess	B20F*	1987-90 1068 ex New Enterprise, 1992 *1068/77/8 are DP19F

1041	E41UKL	1051	E51UKL	1061	E61UKL	1070	G70PKR	1079	G79SKR
1042	E42UKL	1052	E52UKL	1062	E62UKL	1071	G71PKR	1080	G80SKR
1043	E43UKL	1053	E53UKL	1063	E63UKL	1072	G72PKR	1081	G81SKR
1044	E44UKL	1054	E54UKL	1064	E64UKL	1073	G73PKR	1082	G82SKR
1045	E45UKL	1055	E55UKL	1065	E65XKE	1074	G74PKR	1083	G83SKR
1046	E46UKL	1056	E56UKL	1066	F66BKK	1075	G75PKR	1084	G84SKR
1047	E47UKL	1057	E57UKL	1067	F67BKK	1076	G76PKR	1085	G85SKR
1048	E48UKL	1058	E58UKL	1068	F68BKK	1077	G77PKR	1086	G86SKR
1049	E49UKL	1059	E59UKL	1069	G69PKR	1078	G78SKR	1087	G87SKR
1050	E50UKL	1060	E60UKL						

1200	E980NMK	Mercedes-Benz 709D	Reeve Burgess	B20F	1988	Ex Biss, Bishops Stortford, 1990
1201	G201RKK	Mercedes-Benz 709D	Reeve Burgess Beaver	B25F	1989	
1202	G202RKK	Mercedes-Benz 709D	Reeve Burgess Beaver	B25F	1989	
1203	G203RKK	Mercedes-Benz 709D	Reeve Burgess Beaver	B25F	1989	
1204	H204EKO	Mercedes-Benz 709D	Carlyle	B25F	1991	
1401	H395GKO	OBC Omni	OBC	B20F	1991	On extended loan from Kent CC
1402	J110LKO	OBC Omni	OBC	B20F	1991	On extended loan from Kent CC
2142	OKE142P	Leyland Leopard PSU3C/4R	Duple Dominant	C47F	1976	
2159	GGM69W	Leyland Leopard PSU3F/4R	Plaxton Supreme IV Express	C49F	1981	Ex The Bee Line, 1992
2160	GGM72W	Leyland Leopard PSU3F/4R	Plaxton Supreme IV Express	C49F	1981	Ex The Bee Line, 1992
2161	YSU870	Leyland Leopard PSU3E/4RT	Duple Dominant II Express	C49F	1980	
2162	YSU871	Leyland Leopard PSU3E/4RT	Duple Dominant II Express	C49F	1980	
2163	YSU872	Leyland Leopard PSU3E/4RT	Duple Dominant II Express	C49F	1980	
2164	YSU873	Leyland Leopard PSU3E/4R	Duple Dominant II	C53F	1981	Ex New Enterprise, 1990
2167	CKE167Y	Leyland Leopard PSU3G/4R	Eastern Coach Works B51	C49F	1982	
2168	CKE168Y	Leyland Leopard PSU3G/4R	Eastern Coach Works B51	C49F	1982	
2169	CKE169Y	Leyland Leopard PSU3G/4R	Eastern Coach Works B51	C49F	1982	
2170	CKE170Y	Leyland Leopard PSU3G/4R	Eastern Coach Works B51	C49F	1982	
2171	YSU894	Leyland Tiger TRCTL11/2RH	Plaxton Paramount 3200 E	C53F	1983	Ex Kentish Bus, 1990
2172	YSU895	Leyland Tiger TRCTL11/2RH	Plaxton Paramount 3200 E	C53F	1983	Ex London Buses, 1990
2173	YSU896	Leyland Tiger TRCTL11/2RH	Plaxton Paramount 3200 E	C53F	1984	Ex London Country NE, 1990
2174	YSU897	Leyland Tiger TRCTL11/2RH	Plaxton Paramount 3200 E	C53F	1984	Ex Kentish Bus, 1990

2176-2185 — Leyland Tiger TRCTL11/3R, Duple Laser Express, C50F*, 1983, *2179/80/2/5 are C53F, 2181 is C51F

2176 YLK281	2178 681CXM	2180 YOT607	2182 VAY879	2184 544XVW
2177 445YMU	2179 869SVX	2181 NTK611	2183 TSU636	2185 648WHK

2190	ESK987	Leyland Tiger TRCTL11/3R	Duple Caribbean 2	C50F	1985	Ex Brighton & Hove, 1992
2191	ESK988	Leyland Tiger TRCTL11/3R	Duple Caribbean 2	C50F	1985	Ex Brighton & Hove, 1992

2832-2837 — Leyland Leopard PSU3F/4R, Willowbrook 003 II, C47F, 1982

2832 VKN832X	2834 VKN834X	2835 VKN835X	2836 VKN836X	2837 VKN837X

3045	F45ENF	Leyland Lynx LX112L10ZR1R	Leyland	B49F	1988	Ex Shearings, 1991
3046	F46ENF	Leyland Lynx LX112L10ZR1R	Leyland	B49F	1988	Ex Shearings, 1991
3047	F47ENF	Leyland Lynx LX112L10ZR1R	Leyland	B49F	1988	Ex Shearings, 1991
3048	F48ENF	Leyland Lynx LX112L10ZR1R	Leyland	B49F	1988	Ex Shearings, 1991

3445-3462 — Leyland Leopard PSU4B/4R, Marshall, B52F, 1972

3445 EKJ445K	3448 EKJ448K	3452 EKJ452K	3459 GKE459L	3462 GKE462L
3447 EKJ447K	3449 EKJ449K	3456 EKL456K		

3463-3468 — Dennis Dart 9.8SDL3012, Plaxton Pointer, B40F, 1991-92

3463 J463MKL	3465 J465MKL	3466 J466OKP	3467 J467OKP	3468 J468OKP
3464 J464MKL				

3503	NRD147M	Leyland National 1151/1R/0402		B49F	1973	Ex Oxford, 1992
3504	TBL169M	Leyland National 1151/1R/0402		B49F	1974	Ex Oxford, 1992
3505	NEL128P	Leyland National 11351/1R		B49F	1976	Ex Wilts & Dorset, 1992
3506	MAR781P	Leyland National 11351/1R		B49F	1976	Ex Wilts & Dorset, 1992
3521	GKL739N	Leyland National 11351/1R		B49F	1974	
3523	GKL741N	Leyland National 11351/1R		B49F	1974	

3546-3563 — Leyland National 11351A/1R, B49F, 1976-77

3546 PKP546R	3550 PKP550R	3553 PKP553R	3558 SKR558R	3561 VKE561S
3547 PKP547R	3551 PKP551R	3555 SKR555R	3559 VKE559S	3563 VKE563S
3548 PKP548R	3552 PKP552R	3556 SKR556R	3560 VKE560S	

3901-3909 — Leyland National 11351A/1R, DP48F, 1977

3901 SKN901R	3904 SKN904R	3905 SKN905R	3908 SKN908R	3909 SKN909R
3903 SKN903R				

4155	CKR155T	Leyland Leopard PSU3E/4RT	Duple Dominant II	C49F	1979	Ex New Enterprise, 1992
4414	545XFM	Leyland Leopard PSU5C/4R	Duple Dominant I	C51F	1977	Ex New Enterprise, 1992
5021	THM658M	Daimler Fleetline CRL6	MCW	H45/32F	1974	Ex LTE, 1982
5025	GHM830N	Daimler Fleetline CRL6	MCW	H45/32F	1975	Ex New Enterprise, 1988

5026-5033 — Leyland Fleetline FE30ALR, Park Royal, H44/32F, 1976, Ex LTE, 1982

5026 KJD66P	5029 KJD87P	5031 KJD90P	5032 KJD106P	5033 KJD119P
5028 KJD72P	5030 KJD88P			

5035	KUC947P	Daimler Fleetline CRL6	MCW	H44/32F	1975	Ex LTE, 1982
5037	KUC955P	Daimler Fleetline CRL6	MCW	H45/32F	1975	Ex LTE, 1982
5038	KUC957P	Daimler Fleetline CRL6	MCW	H45/32F	1975	Ex LTE, 1982
5039	KUC958P	Daimler Fleetline CRL6	MCW	H45/32F	1975	Ex LTE, 1982
5040	KUC971P	Leyland Fleetline FE30ALR	MCW	H45/32F	1976	Ex LTE, 1982
5041	JDB108N	Daimler Fleetline CRG6LXB	Northern Counties	H43/32F	1975	Ex London Buslines, 1992
5042	HJA117N	Daimler Fleetline CRG6LXB	Northern Counties	H43/32F	1975	Ex London Buslines, 1992
5105	KKO105P	Bristol VRT/SL3/501	Eastern Coach Works	H43/31F	1975	

5107-5116 — Bristol VRT/SL3/6LXB, Eastern Coach Works, H43/31F, 1976

5107 PKM107R	5109 PKM109R	5111 PKM111R	5113 PKM113R	5116 PKM116R
5108 PKM108R	5110 PKM110R	5112 PKM112R	5114 PKM114R	

| 5120 | PKP120R | Bristol VRT/SL3/501 | | Eastern Coach Works | | H43/31F | 1977 | | |

5125-5139

Bristol VRT/SL3/6LXB — Eastern Coach Works — H43/31F — 1977-78

5125	WKO125S	5127	WKO127S	5132	WKO132S	5135	WKO135S	5138	WKO138S
5126	WKO126S	5128	WKO128S	5133	WKO133S	5137	WKO137S	5139	WKO139S

5201-5210

MCW Metrobus 2 DR102/42 — MCW — H46/31F — 1984

5201	A201OKJ	5203	A203OKJ	5205	A205OKJ	5207	A207OKJ	5209	A209OKJ
5202	A202OKJ	5204	A204OKJ	5206	A206OKJ	5208	A208OKJ	5210	A210OKJ

5266	FKM266V	MCW Metrobus DR101/10		MCW		H46/30F	1980		
5270	FKM270V	MCW Metrobus DR104/2		MCW		H46/30F	1980		
5300	XBF700S	Dennis Dominator DD102		Alexander AL		H43/31F	1978	Ex Potteries, 1983	

5301-5306

Dennis Dominator DD129 — Willowbrook — H43/31F — 1980

5301	FKM301V	5303	FKM303V	5304	FKM304V	5305	FKM305V	5306	FKM306V
5302	FKM302V								

5307-5315

Dennis Dominator DD101A* — East Lancashire — H43/32F — 1978-80 Ex East Staffordshire, 1985
*5309/10 are DD110A, 5312-5 are DD120A

5307	XRF22S	5309	FBF127T	5312	PRE35W	5314	PRE38W	5315	PRE39W
5308	XRF23S	5310	FBF128T	5313	PRE36W				

5316	WWM919W	Dennis Dominator DD120B		Willowbrook		H45/33F	1980	Ex Merseybus, 1986	
5317	WWM904W	Dennis Dominator DD120B		Willowbrook		H45/33F	1980	Ex Merseybus, 1986	
5318	UBG24V	Dennis Dominator DD120B		Willowbrook		H45/33F	1980	Ex Merseybus, 1986	

5441-5445

Leyland Olympian ONTL11/2R — Eastern Coach Works — CH45/28F — 1983 5445 rebodied 1985

5441	GKE441Y	5442	GKE442Y	5443	YSU865	5444	YSU866	5445	YSU867

5446	WSU475	Leyland Olympian ONTL11/2RSp		Eastern Coach Works		CH45/28F	1985		
5447	WSU476	Leyland Olympian ONTL11/2RSp		Eastern Coach Works		CH45/28F	1985		
5706	FKM706L	Leyland Atlantean PDR1A/1Sp		MCW		O45/33F	1972		
5708	FKM708L	Leyland Atlantean PDR1A/1Sp		MCW		H45/33F	1972		

5721-5735

Leyland Atlantean AN68A/1R — Northern Counties — H43/32F — 1976-77 Ex GM Buses, 1987-88

5721	LJA621P	5724	LJA650P	5727	SRJ743R	5730	UNA798S	5733	LJA652P
5722	LJA626P	5725	ONF679R	5728	SRJ746R	5731	LJA635P	5734	ONF654R
5723	LJA644P	5726	ONF680R	5729	SRJ751R	5732	LJA648P	5735	ONF655R

5736	KPJ262W	Leyland Atlantean AN68B/1R		Roe		H43/30F	1981	Ex Luton & District, 1991	
5737	KPJ264W	Leyland Atlantean AN68B/1R		Roe		H43/30F	1981	Ex Luton & District, 1991	
5738	KPJ280W	Leyland Atlantean AN68B/1R		Roe		H43/30F	1981	Ex Luton & District, 1991	
5739	KPJ289W	Leyland Atlantean AN68B/1R		Roe		H43/30F	1981	Ex Luton & District, 1991	
5740	MUA862P	Leyland Atlantean AN68/1R		Roe		H43/30F	1975	Ex Luton & District, 1992	
5741	XPG161T	Leyland Atlantean AN68A/1R		Park Royal		H43/30F	1978	Ex Luton & District, 1992	
5742	XPG164T	Leyland Atlantean AN68A/1R		Park Royal		H43/30F	1978	Ex Luton & District, 1992	

5831-5857

Bristol VRT/SL3/6LXB — Eastern Coach Works — H43/31F — 1978-79

5831	BKE831T	5838	BKE838T	5842	BKE842T	5847	BKE847T	5854	BKE854T
5832	BKE832T	5839	BKE839T	5843	BKE843T	5848	BKE848T	5855	BKE855T
5833	BKE833T	5840	BKE840T	5845	BKE845T	5852	BKE852T	5856	BKE856T
5835	BKE835T	5841	BKE841T	5846	BKE846T	5853	BKE853T	5857	BKE857T
5837	BKE837T								

5863-5886

Bristol VRT/SL3/6LXB — Eastern Coach Works — H43/31F — 1979-80

5863	FKM863V	5868	FKM868V	5875	FKM875V	5879	FKM879V	5883	HKM883V
5864	FKM864V	5869	FKM869V	5876	FKM876V	5880	FKM880V	5884	HKM884V
5865	FKM865V	5873	FKM873V	5877	FKM877V	5881	FKM881V	5885	HKM885V
5866	FKM866V	5874	FKM874V	5878	FKM878V	5882	FKM882V	5886	HKM886V
5867	FKM867V								

5888	A888PKR	Leyland Olympian ONLXB/1R	Eastern Coach Works	DPH42/27F	1984
5889	A889PKR	Leyland Olympian ONLXB/1R	Eastern Coach Works	DPH42/27F	1984
5890	A890PKR	Leyland Olympian ONLXB/1R	Eastern Coach Works	DPH42/27F	1984

5891-5900

Leyland Olympian ON6LXB/1RH Northern Counties   H45/30F   1988

| 5891 | E891AKN | 5893 | F893BKK | 5895 | F895BKK | 5897 | F897DKK | 5899 | F899DKK |
| 5892 | F892BKK | 5894 | F894BKK | 5896 | F896DKK | 5898 | F898DKK | 5900 | F900DKK |

5901-5905

Leyland Olympian ON2R50G13Z4 Northern Counties   H45/30F   1990

| 5901 | G901SKP | 5902 | G902SKP | 5903 | G903SKP | 5904 | G904SKP | 5905 | G905SKP |

New Enterprise fleet:

3	A529SRP	Ford Transit	Chassis Developments	B12F	1983	Ex Sapwell, Ashton, 1992
4	H301FKL	Mercedes-Benz 811D	Reeve Burgess Beaver	DP25F	1991	
7	MPL126W	Leyland Leopard PSU3E/4R	Duple Dominant IV Exp (1983)	C53F	1981	Ex Barrie, Alexandria, 1988
8	MPL134W	Leyland Leopard PSU3E/4R	Duple Dominant IV Express	C53F	1981	Ex Barrie, Alexandria, 1988
10	BKJ151T	Leyland Leopard PSU3E/4R	Duple Dominant I Exp	C49F	1979	Ex Maidstone fleet, 1991
12	JKM166V	Leyland Leopard PSU5C/4R	Duple Dominant II	C53F	1980	Ex Maidstone fleet, 1988
14	AKP430T	Bedford YMT	Plaxton Supreme	C53F	1979	Ex Sonner, Gillingham, 1981
15	BNO702T	Bedford YMT	Duple Dominant II Express	C53F	1979	Ex Limebourne, London SW1, 1985
16	CVA110V	Bedford YMT	Plaxton Supreme IV	C45F	1980	Ex Young, Rampton, 1985
18	LSK643	Bedford YNV	Plaxton Paramount 3200 II	C49F	1986	Ex Excelsior, Bournemouth, 1988
20	TSU644	Leyland Tiger TRCTL11/3R	Plaxton Paramount 3200 E	C53F	1983	Ex Maidstone fleet, 1989
23	TSU645	Leyland Tiger TRCTL11/3R	Plaxton Paramount 3200 E	C53F	1983	Ex Maidstone fleet, 1990
24	494WYA	Leyland Tiger TRCTL11/3R	Plaxton Paramount 3500	C57F	1984	Ex PMT, 1990
25	LSK641	Leyland Tiger TRCTL11/3R	Plaxton Paramount 3200	C57F	1983	Ex Mercer, Preston, 1991
26	JUR818V	Bedford YMT	Duple Dominant II	C53F	1979	Ex Ranger, Croydon, 1992
27	4066KO	Scania K92CRB	Plaxton Paramount 3500 II	C55F	1986	Ex Boro'line, 1992
28	642WKR	Bedford YNT	Duple Laser	C53F	1984	Ex Boro'line, 1992
54	THM614M	Daimler Fleetline CRL6	MCW	H44/28D	1974	Ex Keenan, Coalhall, 1987
55	KJD69P	Leyland Fleetline FE30ALR	Park Royal	H43/32F	1976	Ex Maidstone fleet, 1990

Previous Registrations:

445YMU	A177MKE		LSK643	C112AFX		YSU865	GKE443Y
494WYA	A268MEH, 507EXA,		NTK611	A181MKE		YSU866	GKE444Y
	A420HND		TSU636	A183MKE		YSU867	GKE445Y
544XVW	A184MKE		TSU644	FKL174Y		YSU870	JKK161V
545XFM	UKR144S		TSU645	FKL173Y		YSU871	JKK162V
642WHR	B202XKM		TSU646	FKL175Y		YSU872	JKK163V
648WHK	A185MKE		VAY879	A182MKE		YSU873	XGS771X
681CXM	A178MKE		WSU475	B446WKE		YSU894	A107EPA
869SVX	A179MKE		WSU476	B447WKE		YSU895	A114EPA
ESK987	B812JPN		YLK281	A176MKE		YSU896	A135EPA
ESK988	B815JPN		YOT607	A180MKE		YSU897	A140EPA
LSK641	KGS494Y						

Special Liveries:
Invictaway: 2161-3/7-70/2/4/6/7/9-83/90/1,5443-7.
Kent Karrier: 1401/2
Olan Line: 2171/3
Sainsbury's: 5866
Tesco: 5877
Overall Advertisements: 1010/9/26/34/5/52/4/64, 3447, 3559, 5139, 5210, 5842/7/55/63.

On order:
2 Dennis Dart / Plaxton Pointer for 1992 and 5 Leyland Olympian / Northern Counties for 1993.

OXFORD Fleet List

19-24

Leyland Leopard PSU3E/4R   Duple Dominant II Express   C49F   1979

| 19 | YFC19V | 21 | BBW21V | 22 | BBW22V | 23 | BBW23V | 24 | BBW24V |
| 20 | BBW20V | | | | | | | | |

No.	Reg.	Chassis	Body	Seating	Year	Notes
25	MUD25W	Leyland Leopard PSU3F/4R	Duple Dominant IV Express	C49F	1981	
31	VUD31X	Leyland Leopard PSU3G/4R	Eastern Coach Works B51	C49F	1982	

50-55

Dennis Javelin 12SDA1907 — Plaxton Premiére — C53F — 1992

50	K750UJD	52	K752UJD	53	K753UJD	54	K754UJD	55	K755UJD
51	K751UJD								

103-110

Leyland Tiger TRCTL11/3R — Duple Dominant IV Express — C50F — 1983

103	EBW103Y	105	EBW105Y	107	EBW107Y	109	EBW109Y	110	EBW110Y
104	EBW104Y	106	EBW106Y	108	EBW108Y				

No.	Reg.	Chassis	Body	Seating	Year
111	A111MUD	Leyland Tiger TRCTL11/3RH	Plaxton Paramount 3200	C51F	1984
112	A112MUD	Leyland Tiger TRCTL11/3RH	Plaxton Paramount 3200	C51F	1984
113	A113MUD	Leyland Tiger TRCTL11/3RH	Plaxton Paramount 3200	C51F	1984
114	A114MUD	Leyland Tiger TRCTL11/3RH	Plaxton Paramount 3200	C51F	1984

115-119

Leyland Tiger TRCTL11/3RH — Plaxton Paramount 3200 — C51F — 1984

115	A115PBW	116	A116PBW	117	A117PBW	118	A118PBW	119	A119PBW

120-124

Leyland Tiger TRCTL11/3RH — Plaxton Paramount 3200 II — C51F — 1984

120	B120UUD	121	B121UUD	122	B122UUD	123	B123UUD	124	B124UUD

130-134

DAF MB230LT615 — Plaxton Paramount 3500 III — C53F — 1988

130	E130YUD	131	E131YUD	132	E132YUD	133	E133YUD	134	E134YUD

135-139

DAF SB3000DKV601 — Plaxton Paramount 3500 III — C53F — 1989

135	F135LJO	136	F136LJO	137	F137LJO	138	F138LJO	139	F139LJO

No.	Reg.	Chassis	Body	Seating	Year
140	J140NJO	DAF SB2305DHS585	Plaxton Paramount 3200 III	C53F	1991
141	J141NJO	DAF SB2305DHS585	Plaxton Paramount 3200 III	C53F	1991

201-224

Leyland Olympian ONLXB/1R* — Eastern Coach Works — H45/28D — 1982-83   *221 is ONLXC/1R

201	VJO201X	206	VJO206X	211	WWL211X	216	BBW216Y	221	CUD221Y
202	VJO202X	207	WWL207X	212	WWL212X	217	BBW217Y	222	CUD222Y
203	VJO203X	208	WWL208X	213	BBW213Y	218	BBW218Y	223	CUD223Y
204	VJO204X	209	WWL209X	214	BBW214Y	219	CUD219Y	224	CUD224Y
205	VJO205X	210	WWL210X	215	BBW215Y	220	CUD220Y		

225-229

Leyland Olympian ONLXB/1RH — Alexander RL — H47/26D — 1988

225	E225CFC	226	E226CFC	227	E227CFC	228	E228CFC	229	E229CFC

230-235

Leyland Olympian ON2R50G16Z4 — Alexander RL — H47/26D — 1990

230	G230VWL	232	G232VWL	233	G233VWL	234	G234VWL	235	G235VWL
231	G231VWL								

No.	Reg.	Chassis	Body	Seating	Year	Notes
236	FWL778Y	Leyland Olympian ONLXB/1R	Eastern Coach Works	H45/32F	1983	Ex UKAEA, Harwell, 1991
237	FWL779Y	Leyland Olympian ONLXB/1R	Eastern Coach Works	H45/32F	1983	Ex UKAEA, Harwell, 1991
238	FWL780Y	Leyland Olympian ONLXB/1R	Eastern Coach Works	H45/32F	1983	Ex UKAEA, Harwell, 1991
239	FWL781Y	Leyland Olympian ONLXB/1R	Eastern Coach Works	H45/32F	1983	Ex UKAEA, Harwell, 1991
301	OFC901H	Bristol VRT/SL2/6G	Eastern Coach Works	O39/31F	1970	

474-515

Bristol VRT/SL3/6LXB — Eastern Coach Works — H43/27D — 1978-81

474	HUD474S	482	OUD482T	495	HUD495W	502	KJO502W	509	KJO509W
475	HUD475S	483	OUD483T	496	HUD496W	503	KJO503W	510	KJO510W
476	HUD476S	484	OUD484T	497	HUD497W	504	KJO504W	511	PFC511W
477	HUD477S	485	OUD485T	498	HUD498W	505	KJO505W	512	PFC512W
478	HUD478S	486	OUD486T	499	HUD499W	506	KJO506W	513	PFC513W
479	HUD479S	493	HUD493W	500	HUD500W	507	KJO507W	514	PFC514W
480	HUD480S	494	HUD494W	501	HUD501W	508	KJO508W	515	PFC515W
481	HUD481S								

No.	Reg.	Chassis	Body	Seating	Year	Notes
611	RFC11T	Leyland Leopard PSU3E/4R	Willowbrook Warrior (1991)	B48F	1978	
612	WPD27Y	Leyland Leopard PSU3G/4R	Willowbrook Warrior (1991)	B48F	1982	Ex The Bee Line, 1990

613	RFC13T	Leyland Leopard PSU3E/4R	Willowbrook Warrior (1991)	B48F	1978			
614	RFC14T	Leyland Leopard PSU3E/4R	Willowbrook Warrior (1991)	B48F	1978			
627	MUD27W	Leyland Leopard PSU3E/4R	Willowbrook Warrior (1990)	B48F	1981			
633	VUD33X	Leyland Leopard PSU3G/4R	Willowbrook Warrior (1990)	B48F	1982			

750-762

MCW MetroRider MF150 — MCW — B25F — 1987

750	D750SJO	753	E753VJO	756	E756VJO	759	E759XWL	761	E761XWL
751	E751VJO	754	E754VJO	757	E757VJO	760	E760XWL	762	E762XWL
752	E752VJO	755	E755VJO	758	E758XWL				

763	F763LBW	MCW MetroRider MF150/20	MCW	B25F	1989

764-768

MCW MetroRider MF150 — MCW — B23F — 1989 — Ex Merthyr Tydfil, 1989

764	F501ANY	765	F502ANY	766	F503ANY	767	F504ANY	768	F505CBO

769-783

Optare MetroRider — Optare — B28F — 1990

769	G769WFC	772	G772WFC	775	G775WFC	778	G778WFC	781	G781WFC
770	G770WFC	773	G773WFC	776	G776WFC	779	G779WFC	782	G782WFC
771	G771WFC	774	G774WFC	777	G777WFC	780	G780WFC	783	G783WFC

901-905

MCW Metroliner DR130/7 — MCW — CH53/23F — 1985

901	B901XJO	902	B902XJO	903	B903XJO	904	B904XJO	905	B905XJO

906	C906GUD	MCW Metroliner DR130/21	MCW	CH53/23F	1986
907	C907GUD	MCW Metroliner DR130/21	MCW	CH53/23F	1986
908	C908GUD	MCW Metroliner DR130/21	MCW	CH53/23F	1986

975-987

Leyland Atlantean AN68/1R — Eastern Coach Works — H45/27D — 1975 — Ex Northern, 1986-87

975	MPT305P	983	MPT313P	984	MPT314P	986	MPT316P	987	MPT317P

999	PWL999W	Leyland Olympian B45/TL11/2R	Alexander RL	H50/34D	1980	Ex Leyland Motors, 1987

1321-1353

Leyland National 11351/1R — B49F — 1974-75 Ex The Bee Line, 1990

1321	TBL165M	1328	TBL172M	1344	KPA357P	1351	KPA377P	1353	KPA384P
1327	TBL171M	1335	GPC734N	1346	KPA359P				

1354-1384

Leyland National 11351A/1R — B49F* — 1976-78 Ex The Bee Line, 1990
*1378 is DP21FL, 1384 is DP45F

1354	KPA390P	1356	NPJ481R	1360	TPE158S	1378	TPE170S	1384	VPF296S

1401-1405

Leyland Lynx LX112L10ZR1S — Leyland — B49F — 1988 Ex The Bee Line, 1990

1401	F556NJM	1402	F557NJM	1403	F558NJM	1404	F559NJM	1405	F560NJM

1508	MRJ8W	Bristol VRT/SL3/6LXB	Eastern Coach Works	DPH41/29F	1980	Ex Mayne, Manchester, 1991
1509	MRJ9W	Bristol VRT/SL3/6LXB	Eastern Coach Works	DPH41/29F	1980	Ex Mayne, Manchester, 1991

1534-1557

Bristol VRT/SL3/6LXB — Eastern Coach Works — H43/31F — 1976 Ex The Bee Line, 1990

1534	GGM76W	1544	HJB451W	1548	HJB455W	1552	HJB459W	1555	HJB462W
1541	GGM108W	1545	HJB452W	1549	HJB456W	1553	HJB460W	1556	HJB463W
1542	GGM109W	1546	HJB453W	1550	HJB457W	1554	HJB461W	1557	HJB464W
1543	GGM110W	1547	HJB454W	1551	HJB458W				

1563	CJH124V	Bristol VRT/SL3/6LXB	Eastern Coach Works	DPH41/25F	1980	Ex The Bee Line, 1990
1726	MUD26W	Leyland Leopard PSU3F/4R	Duple Dominant IV Express	C49F	1981	
1757	YPJ209Y	Leyland Tiger TRCTL11/3R	Plaxton Paramount 3500	C50F	1983	Ex The Bee Line, 1990
1763	A213DPB	Leyland Tiger TRCTL11/3RH	Plaxton Paramount 3200	C51F	1983	Ex The Bee Line, 1990
1822	D822UTF	Leyland Olympian ONLXB/1RH	Eastern Coach Works	CH39/21F	1986	Ex The Bee Line, 1990
1823	D823UTF	Leyland Olympian ONLXB/1RH	Eastern Coach Works	CH39/21F	1986	Ex The Bee Line, 1990
1824	D824UTF	Leyland Olympian ONLXB/1RH	Eastern Coach Works	CH39/21F	1986	Ex The Bee Line, 1990

Special Liveries:
Park & Ride: 225-9, 999

PEOPLES PROVINCIAL Fleet List

1	A301KJT	Leyland National 2 NL116L11/1R			DP47F	1984
2	A302KJT	Leyland National 2 NL116L11/1R			DP47F	1984

13-22 — Leyland National 1151/2R/0403 — B44D — 1972-74

13	HOR413L	15	HOR415L	17	HOR417L	19	PCG919M	21	PCG921M
14	HOR414L	16	HOR416L	18	PCG918M	20	PCG920M	22	PCG922M

23	RUF37R	Leyland National 11351A/2R		B44D	1977	Ex Rennies, Dunfirmline, 1988

24-33 — Leyland National 11351/2R — B44D — 1974-75

24	UAA224M	27	GCR727N	29	JBP129P	31	JBP131P	33	JBP133P
26	UAA226M	28	GCR728N	30	JBP130P	32	JBP132P		

34-44 — Leyland National 11351A/2R — B44D — 1976-79 43/4 are B26D

34	LTP634P	37	MOW637R	39	PTR239S	41	TPX41T	43	UPO443T
35	LTP635P	38	PTR238S	40	SBK740S	42	TPX42T	44	UPO444T
36	MOW636R								

51	NPD130L	Leyland National 1151/1R/0402	B49F	1973	Ex London Country, 1983
52	NPD131L	Leyland National 1151/1R/0402	B49F	1973	Ex London Country, 1983
53	NPD132L	Leyland National 1151/1R/0402	B49F	1973	Ex London Country, 1983
63	MJT880P	Leyland National 11351/1R	B49F	1976	Ex Hants & Dorset, 1983
64	KDW338P	Leyland National 11351/1R	B49F	1976	Ex National Welsh, 1987

65-72 — Leyland National 11351A/1R — B49F — 1977-78 Ex Hants & Dorset, 1983

65	RTJ147R	67	SPR39R	70	UFX847S	71	UFX848S	72	VFX980S
66	RTJ148R	68	SPR40R						

73	EEL893V	Leyland National 11351A/1R	DP52F	1979	Ex Hants & Dorset, 1983
74	GLJ674N	Leyland National 11351/1R	B48F	1974	Ex Hants & Dorset, 1983
76	WFX257S	Leyland National 11351A/1R	DP48F	1978	Ex Hants & Dorset, 1983

118-127 — Iveco Daily 49.10 — Robin Hood — B19F — 1986 — 127 is B21F

118	D118DRV	120	D120DRV	122	D122DRV	123	D123DRV	127	D127DRV
119	D119DRV	121	D121DRV						

128-139 — Iveco Daily 49.10 — Pheonix — B24F — 1989

128	F128SBP	131	F131SBP	134	F134TCR	136	F136TCR	138	G138WOW
129	F129SBP	132	F132SBP	135	F135TCR	137	G137WOW	139	G139WOW

140-146 — Iveco Daily 49.101 — Marshall — B23F — 1992

140	J140KPX	142	J142KPX	144	J144KPX	145	J145KPX	146	J146KPX
141	J141KPX	143	J143KPX						

204	UGR701R	Bristol VRT/SL3/6LXB	Eastern Coach Works	H43/31F	1976	Ex Northumbria, 1989
206	UGR706R	Bristol VRT/SL3/6LXB	Eastern Coach Works	H43/31F	1976	Ex Northumbria, 1989
207	UGR707R	Bristol VRT/SL3/6LXB	Eastern Coach Works	H43/31F	1976	Ex Northumbria, 1989
208	AUP715S	Bristol VRT/SL3/6LXB	Eastern Coach Works	H43/31F	1977	Ex Northumbria, 1989
303	NFN79M	Leyland National 1151/1R/2402		B49F	1974	Ex National Welsh, 1987
305	NPD146L	Leyland National 1151/1R/0402		B49F	1973	Ex London Country, 1983
306	NPD154L	Leyland National 1151/1R/0402		B49F	1973	Ex London Country, 1983
333	H523CTR	ACE Cougar	Wadham Stringer Vanguard	B41F	1990	Ex W S demonstrator, 1991
350	NPD128L	Leyland National 1151/1R/0402		B49F	1973	Ex London Country, 1983

355-361 — Leyland National 11351/1R — B52F — 1974 Ex National Welsh, 1987

355	GHB684N	356	GHB789N	359	HTG470N	360	KDW330P	361	KDW334P

369	SPR41R	Leyland National 11351A/1R	B49F	1977	Ex Hants & Dorset, 1983
375	WFX253S	Leyland National 11351A/1R	DB48F	1978	Ex Hants & Dorset, 1983
377	KDW340P	Leyland National 11351/1R	B49F	1975	Ex National Welsh, 1987
378	KDW343P	Leyland National 11351/1R	B49F	1976	Ex National Welsh, 1987

379	NWO480R	Leyland National 11351A/1R		B49F	1976	Ex National Welsh, 1987
381	NPD135L	Leyland National 1151/1R/0402		B49F	1973	Ex London Country, 1983
382	PHA491M	Leyland National 11351/1R		B49F	1974	Ex Midland Red East, 1983
383	NOE561R	Leyland National 11351A/1R		B49F	1976	Ex Midland Red East, 1983
384	PUK642R	Leyland National 11351A/1R		B49F	1977	Ex Midland Red East, 1983
385	NPD134L	Leyland National 1151/1R/0402		B49F	1973	Ex London Country, 1983
386	NWO490R	Leyland National 11351A/1R		B49F	1976	Ex National Welsh, 1987
387	NWO498R	Leyland National 11351A/1R		B49F	1977	Ex National Welsh, 1987
388	PKG735R	Leyland National 11351A/1R		B49F	1977	Ex National Welsh, 1987
389	SKG919S	Leyland National 11351A/1R		B49F	1977	Ex National Welsh, 1987

390-394
Leyland National 1151/1R/0102 — B49F — 1973 — Ex Southdown, 1988

390	BCD817L	391	BCD818L	392	BCD819L	393	BCD821L	394	BCD824L

396	HTX726N	Leyland National 11351/1R		B49F	1975	Ex Rennies, Dunfirmline, 1988

401-414
Leyland National 10351A/2R — B36D — 1976-79 — Ex London Buses, 1991

401	KJD528P	404	AYR331T	407	THX234S	410	THX115S	413	AYR341T
402	THX248S	405	AYR344T	408	BYW415V	411	THX131S	414	YYE276T
403	AYR299T	406	YYE278T	409	KJD511P	412	THX242S		

591	NFX130P	Leyland Fleetline FE30LR	Alexander AD	CO43/31F	1976	Ex Yellow Buses, 1991
592	NFX131P	Leyland Fleetline FE30LR	Alexander AD	CO43/31F	1976	Ex Yellow Buses, 1991

Special Liveries:
Overall Advertisements: 65/8, 71, 84, 388, 405/13.

READING TRANSPORT Fleet List

11	E911DRD	Leyland Olympian ONLXCT/1RH	Optare	H42/26D	1988
12	E912DRD	Leyland Olympian ONLXCT/1RH	Optare	H42/26D	1988

13-17
Leyland Olympian ONLXB/1RH — Optare — H42/26D — 1988

13	E913DRD	14	E914DRD	15	E915DRD	16	E916DRD	17	E917DRD

68	YJB68T	Leyland Titan TNLXB2RRSp	Park Royal	H44/25D	1979
69	YJB69T	Leyland Titan TNLXB2RRSp	Park Royal	H44/25D	1979

70-74
Leyland Titan TNLXB2RR — Leyland — H44/26D — 1983

70	SBL70Y	71	RMO71Y	72	RMO72Y	73	RMO73Y	74	RMO74Y

75-79
Leyland Titan TNLXC1RF — Leyland — DPH39/27F — 1983

75	RMO75Y	76	RMO76Y	77	RMO77Y	78	RMO78Y	79	RMO79Y

80-84
Leyland Olympian ONLXCT/1RH — Eastern Coach Works — CH39/25F — 1986

80	D80UTF	81	D81UTF	82	D82UTF	83	D83UTF	84	D84UTF

85	F85MJH	Leyland Olympian ONLXCT/1RH	Optare	DPH39/25F	1988
86	F86MJH	Leyland Olympian ONLXCT/1RH	Optare	DPH39/25F	1988
87	F87MJH	Leyland Olympian ONLXCT/1RH	Optare	DPH39/25F	1988

101	C319RPE	Ford Transit 190	Carlyle	B16F	1986	Ex The Bee Line, 1992
104	D825UTF	Ford Transit 190	Carlyle	B16F	1986	Ex The Bee Line, 1992

143-149
MCW Metrobus DR102/44 — MCW — DPH39/27F — 1984

143	A143AMO	145	A145AMO	147	B147EDP	148	B148EDP	149	B149EDP
144	A144AMO	146	A146AMO						

150-165   MCW Metrobus DR102/8   MCW   H43/27D   1979

150	WRD150T	154	WRD154T	157	WRD157T	160	WRD160T	163	WRD163T
151	WRD151T	155	WRD155T	158	WRD158T	161	WRD161T	164	CJH164V
152	WRD152T	156	WRD156T	159	WRD159T	162	WRD162T	165	CJH165V
153	WRD153T								

166-183   MCW Metrobus DR102/16   MCW   H45/27D   1980-81

166	CJH166V	170	CJH170V	174	HCF174W	178	HCF178W	181	HCF181W
167	CJH167V	171	CJH171V	175	HCF175W	179	HCF179W	182	HCF182W
168	CJH168V	172	CJH172V	176	HCF176W	180	HCF180W	183	HCF183W
169	CJH169V	173	HCF173W	177	HCF177W				

184-188   MCW Metrobus DR102/25   MCW   H45/28D   1982

184	LMO184X	185	LMO185X	186	LMO186X	187	LMO187X	188	LMO188X

189-193   MCW Metrobus DR102/30   MCW   DPH43/25D 1982

189	LMO189X	190	LMO190X	191	LMO191X	192	LMO192X	193	LMO193X

201-210   Mercedes-Benz 811D   Optare StarRider   B26F   1988-89 Ex The Bee Line, 1992

201	F531NRD	203	F533NRD	205	F535NRD	207	F361SDP	209	F363SDP
202	F532NRD	204	F534NRD	206	F360SDP	208	F362SDP	210	F364SDP

211	E459CGM	Mercedes-Benz 609D	Robin Hood	B20F	1987	Ex The Bee Line, 1992
212	E460CGM	Mercedes-Benz 609D	Robin Hood	B20F	1987	Ex The Bee Line, 1992
213	E468CGM	Mercedes-Benz 609D	Robin Hood	B20F	1987	Ex The Bee Line, 1992
220	BUS5X	Scania K113CRB	Van Hool Alizée	C49FT	1989	
231	C912YPW	Hestair Duple 425	Duple 425	C55FT	1986	Ex Ambassador Travel, 1991
232	D124FDF	Hestair Duple 425	Duple 425	C55FT	1987	Ex Swanbrook, Cheltenham, 1991
233	E125LAD	Hestair Duple 425	Duple 425	C52FT	1988	Ex Swanbrook, Cheltenham, 1991
241	E205EPB	Hestair Duple 425	Duple 425	C57F	1987	Ex Alder Valley, 1991
242	E209EPB	Hestair Duple 425	Duple 425	C57F	1987	Ex Alder Valley, 1991
243	E210EPB	Hestair Duple 425	Duple 425	C57F	1987	Ex Alder Valley, 1991

244-248   Hestair Duple 425   Duple 425   C55F   1987   Ex The Bee Line, 1991

244	E451CGM	245	E452CGM	246	E453CGM	247	E454CGM	248	E456CGM

307-319   Leyland National 1151/1R/0402   B49F   1973-74 Ex The Bee Line, 1992

307	NRD144M	308	NRD145M	314	NRD155M	318	NRD161M	319	NRD162M

322-343   Leyland National 11351/1R   B49F   1974-75 Ex The Bee Line, 1992

322	TBL166M	333	GPC731N	339	GPJ895N	341	GPJ898N	343	KPA355P
332	GPC730N	334	GPC732N	340	GPJ896N				

357	NPJ483R	Leyland National 11351A/1R		B49F	1976	Ex The Bee Line, 1992
361	TPE147S	Leyland National 11351A/1R		B49F	1976	Ex The Bee Line, 1992
382	LPF603P	Leyland National 11351/1R/SC		DP45F	1976	Ex The Bee Line, 1992
383	TPE171S	Leyland National 11351A/1R		DP45F	1978	Ex The Bee Line, 1992

455-469   MCW Metrobus DR102   MCW   H45/30F   1987   Ex London Buses, 1991

455	E454SON	458	E458SON	461	E247KCF	464	E464SON	467	E467SON
456	E456SON	459	E459SON	462	E462SON	465	E465SON	468	E468SON
457	E457SON	460	E460SON	463	E463SON	466	E466SON	469	E469SON

501-510   DAF SB220LC550   Optare Delta   B49F*   1989   *508 is B44F

501	G501XBL	503	G503XBL	505	G505XBL	507	G507XBL	509	G509XBL
502	G502XBL	504	G504XBL	506	G506XBL	508	G508XBL	510	G510XBL

519-558   Bristol VRT/SL3/6LXB   Eastern Coach Works   H43/31F   1978-80 Ex The Bee Line, 1992

519	VPF284S	522	VPF287S	529	CJH115V	531	CJH118V	536	GGM78W
520	VPF285S	527	CJH141V	530	CJH116V	535	GGM77W	558	GGM79W

564	CJH125V	Bristol VRT/SL3/6LXB	Eastern Coach Works	CH41/25F	1980	Ex The Bee Line, 1992
565	CJH126V	Bristol VRT/SL3/6LXB	Eastern Coach Works	H43/31F	1980	Ex The Bee Line, 1992

573	RTH919S	Bristol VRT/SL3/501	Eastern Coach Works	H43/31F	1977	Ex The Bee Line, 1992
574	RTH921S	Bristol VRT/SL3/501	Eastern Coach Works	H43/31F	1977	Ex The Bee Line, 1992

601-606 MCW MetroRider MF158/8 MCW B31F 1988

601	E601HTF	603	E603HTF	604	E604HTF	605	E605HTF	606	E606HTF
602	E602HTF								

607-613 Optare MetroRider Optare B25F 1991

607	J607SJB	609	J609SJB	611	J611SJB	612	J612SJB	613	H613NJB
608	J608SJB	610	J610SJB						

701	MRD1	DAF DB250HS505	Optare Spectra	H43/28F	1992
702	K702BBL	DAF DB250HS505	Optare Spectra	H43/28F	1992
703	K703BBL	DAF DB250HS505	Optare Spectra	H43/28F	1992
710	GGM64W	Leyland Leopard PSU3F/4R	Plaxton Supreme IV Express	C49F	1981	Ex The Bee Line, 1992
711	GGM65W	Leyland Leopard PSU3F/4R	Plaxton Supreme IV Express	C49F	1981	Ex The Bee Line, 1992
713	GGM68W	Leyland Leopard PSU3F/4R	Plaxton Supreme IV Express	C49F	1981	Ex The Bee Line, 1992
751	YPJ201Y	Leyland Tiger TRCTL11/3R	Plaxton Paramount 3500	C50F	1983	Ex The Bee Line, 1992
756	YPJ208Y	Leyland Tiger TRCTL11/3R	Plaxton Paramount 3500	C50F	1983	Ex The Bee Line, 1992
758	YPJ210Y	Leyland Tiger TRCTL11/3R	Plaxton Paramount 3500	C50F	1983	Ex The Bee Line, 1992
764	A214DPB	Leyland Tiger TRCTL11/3RH	Plaxton Paramount 3200	C51F	1989	Ex The Bee Line, 1992
781	F771OJH	Volvo B10M-61	Jonckheere Jubilee P50	C53F	1989	Ex The Bee Line, 1992
784	F774OJH	Volvo B10M-61	Jonckheere Jubilee P50	C53F	1989	Ex The Bee Line, 1992
785	F775OJH	Volvo B10M-61	Jonckheere Jubilee P50	C53F	1989	

Previous Registrations:
E247KCF   E475SON, MRD1   BUS5X   F220SDP

Special Liveries:
London link   80/2/3, 241-8.
Overall Advertisements: 11/5, 72/4, 87, 185.

Operating Units:
Newbury Buses: 101/4, 201-13, 307/14/8/9/32-4/9/40/57/61/82, 758/81/4/5.
Reading Buses: Remainder

SOUTHAMPTON CITYBUS Fleet List

102	F102RTR	Leyland Lynx LX112L10ZR1S	Leyland	B47F	1989

104-111 Leyland Lynx LX2R11C15Z4R Leyland B47F 1990

104	G104WRV	106	G106WRV	108	G108WRV	110	G110XOW	111	G111XOW
105	G105WRV	107	G107WRV	109	G109XOW				

112	G112XOW	Leyland Lynx LX112L10ZR1R	Leyland	DP47F	1990
113	G113XOW	Leyland Lynx LX112L10ZR1R	Leyland	DP47F	1990
133	TTR167H	Leyland Atlantean PDR1A/1	East Lancashire	H43/13DL	1970
134	TTR168H	Leyland Atlantean PDR1A/1	East Lancashire	H43/13DL	1970

168-200 Leyland Atlantean AN68/1R East Lancashire H45/31F 1972-75

168	EOW401L	174	PCR297M	184	PCR307M	191	HTR561P	195	HTR557P
169	EOW402L	177	PCR300M	187	JBK886P	192	HTR562P	196	HTR565P
171	EOW404L	178	PCR301M	188	HTR558P	193	HTR563P	197	HTR566P
172	PCR295M	182	PCR305M	189	HTR559P	194	HTR564P	200	HTR569P
173	PCR296M	183	PCR306M	190	HTR560P				

202-231 Leyland Atlantean AN68A/1R East Lancashire H45/31F 1977-78

202	MCR202R	208	MCR208R	214	MCR214R	220	PBP220S	226	PBP226S
203	MCR203R	209	MCR209R	215	MCR215R	221	PBP221S	227	PBP227S
204	MCR204R	210	MCR210R	216	MCR216R	222	PBP222S	228	PBP228S
205	MCR205R	211	MCR211R	217	ORV90S	223	PBP223S	229	PBP229S
206	MCR206R	212	MCR212R	218	MCR218R	224	PBP224S	230	PBP230S
207	MCR207R	213	MCR213R	219	ORV89S	225	PBP225S	231	PBP231S

232-261 — Leyland Atlantean AN68A/1R — East Lancashire — H45/31F — 1979-80

232	UPO232T	238	UPO238T	244	UPO244T	250	YRV250V	256	YRV256V
233	UPO233T	239	UPO239T	245	UPO245T	251	YRV251V	257	YRV257V
234	UPO234T	240	UPO240T	246	UPO246T	252	YRV252V	258	YRV258V
235	UPO235T	241	UPO241T	247	YRV247V	253	YRV253V	259	YRV259V
236	UPO236T	242	UPO242T	248	YRV248V	254	YRV254V	260	YRV260V
237	UPO237T	243	UPO243T	249	YRV249V	255	YRV255V	261	YRV261V

262-266 — Leyland Atlantean AN68B/1R — East Lancashire — H45/31F — 1981

262	DBK262W	263	DBK263W	264	DBK264W	265	DBK265W	266	DBK266W

267-276 — Leyland Atlantean AN68C/1R — East Lancashire — H45/31F — 1982

267	FTR267X	269	FTR269X	271	FTR271X	273	KOW273Y	275	KOW275Y
268	FTR268X	270	FTR270X	272	KOW272Y	274	KOW274Y	276	KOW276Y

277	A277ROW	Dennis Dominator DDA171	East Lancashire	H46/30F	1984
289	E289HRV	Leyland Olympian ONLXB/1RH	Eastern Coach Works	DPH43/27F	1987
290	E290HRV	Leyland Olympian ONLXB/1RH	Eastern Coach Works	DPH43/27F	1987

291-298 — Dennis Dominator DDA1023 — East Lancashire — H45/31F — 1988

291	F291PTP	293	F293PTP	295	F295PTP	297	F297PTP	298	F298PTP
292	F292PTP	294	F294PTP	296	F296PTP		

300	GTP95X	Dennis Lancet SD504	Wadham Stringer Vanguard	DP35F	1982	Ex Portsmouth, 1989

301-306 — Dennis Dart 9SDL3002 — Duple Dartline — B36F — 1990 — 306 is B35F

301	G301XCR	303	G303XCR	304	G304XCR	305	G305XCR	306	H306DRV
302	G302XCR						

307	G895XPX	Dennis Dart 8.5SDL3003	Wadham Stringer Vanguard	B33F	1990	Ex W S demonstrator, 1990
308	H308ERV	Dennis Dart 9SDL3002	Reeve Burgess Pointer	B35F	1991	

350-354 — Leyland Atlantean AN68/1R — East Lancashire Sprint (1991) — B35F — 1974

350	OJI1870	351	OJI1871	352	EOW398L	353	HTR570P	354	HTR568P

500	115CLT	Kässbohrer Setra S228DT	Kässbohrer Imperial	CH54/20CT	1984	Ex Harris, Catshill, 1991
501	MJI4605	Kässbohrer Setra S228DT	Kässbohrer Imperial	CH54/20CT	1984	Ex Smith, Bold Heath, 1992
502	C287BBP	Leyland Olympian ONLXCT/2R	East Lancashire	CH47/21FT	1986	
503	C288BBP	Leyland Olympian ONLXCT/2R	East Lancashire	CH47/29F	1986	
504	WLT649	Leyland Olympian ONTL11/2Rsp	East Lancashire	CH49/20FT	1986	Ex London Coaches, 1990
505	C202DYE	Leyland Olympian ONTL11/2Rsp	East Lancashire	CH49/20FT	1986	Ex London Coaches, 1990
507	WOW529J	Leyland Atlantean PDR1A/1	East Lancashire	O45/31F	1971	
511	AUS644S	Leyland Leopard PSU5B/4R	Duple Dominant	C55F	1978	Ex Portsmouth, 1989

Previous Registrations:

115CLT	B149NPE, SWH67	OJI1870	PCR299M	WLT649	C201DYE
MJI4605	A574GEF	OJI1871	HTR567P		

Special Liveries:

Wheels on wheels: 133/4   Red Ensign: 502-5/7/11

SOUTHERN VECTIS/SOLENT BLUE LINE Fleet List

83	NDL653R	Bristol VRT/SL3/6LXB	Eastern Coach Works	H43/31F	1977	
84	NDL654R	Bristol VRT/SL3/6LXB	Eastern Coach Works	H43/31F	1977	
85	RPR715R	Bristol VRT/SL3/6LXB	Eastern Coach Works	H43/31F	1977	Ex Hampshire Bus, 1987
87	RPR717R	Bristol VRT/SL3/6LXB	Eastern Coach Works	H43/31F	1977	Ex Hampshire Bus, 1987
89	VPR489S	Bristol VRT/SL3/6LXB	Eastern Coach Works	H43/31F	1977	Ex Hampshire Bus, 1987
94	RFB614S	Bristol VRT/SL3/6LXB	Eastern Coach Works	H43/31F	1978	Ex Southern Vectis, 1991
96	BFX576T	Bristol VRT/SL3/6LXB	Eastern Coach Works	H43/31F	1979	Ex Hampshire Bus, 1987
97	BFX577T	Bristol VRT/SL3/6LXB	Eastern Coach Works	H43/31F	1979	Ex Hampshire Bus, 1987
102	A295FDL	Leyland Olympian ONLXB/1Rp	Eastern Coach Works	CH41/23F	1984	

149-165 Bristol VRT/SL3/501 Eastern Coach Works H43/31F 1978-79 Ex Cumberland, 1987
Now fitted with Gardner engines

149	LHG449T	153	LHG453T	157	LHG457T	160	TRN460V	163	TRN463V
150	LHG450T	154	LHG454T	158	LHG458T	161	TRN461V	164	TRN464V
151	LHG451T	155	LHG455T	159	LHG459T	162	TRN462V	165	TRN465V
152	LHG452T	156	LHG456T						

202	KDL202W	Bristol LHS6L	Eastern Coach Works	DP31F	1980
203	KDL203W	Bristol LHS6L	Eastern Coach Works	DP31F	1980

205-212 Mercedes-Benz 811D Pheonix B31F 1990

205	G205YDL	207	G207YDL	209	G209YDL	211	G211YDL	212	G212YDL
206	G206YDL	208	G208YDL	210	G210YDL				

224	C224XRU	Ford Transit 190D	Robin Hood	B16F	1985	Ex Hampshire Bus, 1987
225	C225XRU	Ford Transit 190D	Robin Hood	B16F	1985	Ex Hampshire Bus, 1987
226	C226XRU	Ford Transit 190D	Robin Hood	B16F	1985	Ex Hampshire Bus, 1987

231-238 Iveco Daily 49.10 Car Chairs B23F 1992

231	J231KDL	233	J233KDL	235	J235KDL	237	J237KDL	238	J238KDL
232	J232KDL	234	J234KDL	236	J236KDL				

255-268 Ford Transit 190D Carlyle B16F 1985

255	C255SDL	258	B258MDL	263	C263SDL	265	C265SDL	267	C267SDL
257	B257MDL	262	C262SDL	264	C264SDL	266	C266SDL	268	C268SDL

269	D269YDL	Ford Transit 190D	Dormobile	DP18F	1986
270	D270YDL	Ford Transit 190D	Dormobile	B18F	1986

271-287 Iveco Daily 49.10 Robin Hood B19F 1987-89

271	E271HDL	275	E275HDL	279	E279HDL	282	F282ODL	285	F285SDL
272	E272HDL	276	E276HDL	280	F280ODL	283	F283SDL	286	F286SDL
273	E273HDL	277	E277HDL	281	F281ODL	284	F284SDL	287	F287SDL
274	E274HDL	278	E278HDL						

288	G565YTR	Iveco Daily 49.10	Pheonix	B23F	1990	Ex Pheonix demonstrator, 1990
289	H289DDL	Iveco Daily 49.10	Pheonix	B23F	1990	
301	KDL885F	Bristol RESH6G	Duple Commander	C45F	1968	
302	CXI5971	Leyland Leopard PSU3C/4R	Plaxton Supreme	C52F	1979	Ex The Bee Line, 1989
307	LXI4409	Leyland Leopard PSU3F/4R	Plaxton Supreme	C52F	1981	
310	WDL142	Leyland Tiger TRCTL11/3R	Plaxton Paramount 3200	C51F	1983	
311	WDL311Y	Leyland Tiger TRCTL11/3R	Plaxton Paramount 3200	C51F	1983	
312	A312BDL	Leyland Tiger TRCTL11/3R	Plaxton Paramount 3200	C51F	1984	
313	A313BDL	Leyland Tiger TRCTL11/3R	Plaxton Paramount 3200	C51F	1984	
314	WDL748	Leyland Tiger TRCTL11/3R	Plaxton Paramount 3200 II	C47F	1986	
315	473CDL	Leyland Tiger TRCTL11/3R	Plaxton Paramount 3200 II	C51F	1986	
316	390CDL	Leyland Tiger TRCTL11/3R	Plaxton Paramount 3500 II	C47F	1986	
317	VDL263	Leyland Tiger TRCTL11/3R	Plaxton Paramount 3500 II	C51F	1986	
320	E320JDL	Leyland Tiger TRCTL11/3RZ	Plaxton Paramount 3500 III	C53F	1988	
321	E321JDL	Leyland Tiger TRCTL11/3RZ	Plaxton Paramount 3500 III	C53F	1988	
326	934BDL	Leyland Tiger TRCTL11/3R	Plaxton Paramount 3200	C53F	1984	Ex Hill, Tredegar, 1989
402	SEL239N	Leyland National 11351/1R		B49F	1973	Ex Hampshire Bus, 1988
403	SEL240N	Leyland National 11351/1R		B49F	1973	Ex Hampshire Bus, 1988
404	LPR937P	Leyland National 11351/1R		B49F	1973	Ex Hampshire Bus, 1987

406-423 Leyland National 11351A/1R B49F* 1976-80 Ex Hampshire Bus, 1987
*422 is DP48F

406	NEL122P	411	PJT268R	417	UFX852S	420	WPR150S	422	FPR64V
407	NEL123P	412	PJT270R	418	VFX982S	421	DRU7T	423	FPR65V
410	PJT267R	415	UFX849S	419	VFX985S				

428	NEV683M	Leyland National 1151/1R/0402		B49F	1973	Ex Eastern National, 1989
430	JNO198N	Leyland National 11351/1R		B49F	1975	Ex Eastern National, 1989
432	WXI6291	Bedford YMT	Plaxton Supreme	C53F	1979	
501	MDL952	Bristol LD6G	Eastern Coach Works	O33/27R	1956	
502	CDL899	Bristol K5G	Eastern Coach Works	O30/26R	1939	
503	VDL613S	Bristol VRT/SL3/6LXB	Eastern Coach Works	CO43/31F	1977	Ex Hants & Dorset, 1979
504	UFX856S	Bristol VRT/SL3/6LXB	Eastern Coach Works	CO43/31F	1977	Ex Hants & Dorset, 1979

505	UFX857S	Bristol VRT/SL3/6LXB	Eastern Coach Works	CO43/31F	1977	Ex Hants & Dorset, 1979
506	UFX858S	Bristol VRT/SL3/6LXB	Eastern Coach Works	CO43/31F	1977	Ex Hants & Dorset, 1979
509	PTT98R	Bristol VRT/SL3/6LXB	Eastern Coach Works	H43/31F	1976	Ex Devon General, 1987
510	VOD595S	Bristol VRT/SL3/6LXB	Eastern Coach Works	H43/31F	1978	Ex Devon General, 1987
565	TDL998	Bristol FS6G	Eastern Coach Works	H33/27RD	1960	
573	YDL318	Bristol FS6G	Eastern Coach Works	H33/27RD	1962	
611	CDL479C	Bristol FLF6G	Eastern Coach Works	H38/32F	1965	Ex Shamrock & Rambler, 1986
628	SDL638J	Bristol VRT/SL6G	Eastern Coach Works	H39/31F	1971	

660-670

Bristol VRT/SL3/6LXB   Eastern Coach Works   H43/31F   1977-78

660	ODL660R	663	ODL663R	665	ODL665R	667	ODL667R	669	UDL669S
661	ODL661R	664	ODL664R	666	ODL666R	668	UDL668S	670	UDL670S
662	ODL662R								

671-685

Bristol VRT/SL3/6LXB   Eastern Coach Works   H43/31F   1979-81

671	YDL671T	674	YDL674T	677	FDL677V	680	FDL680V	683	DPX683W
672	YDL672T	675	YDL675T	678	FDL678V	681	FDL681V	684	DPX684W
673	YDL673T	676	YDL676T	679	FDL679V	682	FDL682V	685	DPX685W

686-700

Leyland Olympian ONLXB/1R   Eastern Coach Works   H45/30F   1982-84

686	RDL686X	689	RDL689X	692	RDL692X	695	WDL695Y	698	A698DDL
687	RDL687X	690	RDL690X	693	WDL693Y	696	WDL696Y	699	A699DDL
688	RDL688X	691	RDL691X	694	WDL694Y	697	A697DDL	700	A700DDL

701-705

Leyland Olympian ONLXB/1R   Eastern Coach Works   H45/30F   1982   Ex Hampshire Bus, 1987

701	A201MEL	702	A202MEL	703	A203MEL	704	A204MEL	705	A205MEL

706-712

Leyland Olympian ONCL10/1RZ Leyland   DPH39/29F 1989

706	F706SDL	708	F708SDL	710	F710SDL	711	F711SDL	712	F712SDL
707	F707SDL	709	F709SDL						

713-727

Leyland Olympian ON2R50C13Z5 Leyland   DPH43/29F 1989/90

713	G713WDL	716	G716WDL	719	G719WDL	722	G722WDL	725	G725XDL
714	G714WDL	717	G717WDL	720	G720WDL	723	G723XDL	726	G726XDL
715	G715WDL	718	G718WDL	721	G721WDL	724	G724XDL	727	G727XDL

728-734

Leyland Olympian ON2R50C13Z5 Leyland   H47/31F   1991

728	H728DDL	730	H730DDL	732	H732DDL	733	H733DDL	734	H734DDL
729	H729DDL	731	H731DDL						

806	FDL927D	Bristol MW6G	Eastern Coach Works	B45F	1966	Ex Relf, Haselmere, 1989
817	F817URN	Leyland Olympian ONCL10/1RZ	Leyland	H47/31F	1988	Ex Volvo demonstrator, 1990
863	TDL563K	Bristol RELL6G	Eastern Coach Works	B53F	1972	
864	TDL564K	Bristol RELL6G	Eastern Coach Works	O53F	1972	
901	H901EDL	Kässbohrer Setra S215HD	Kässbohrer Tornado	C49F	1991	
902	J902LDL	Kässbohrer Setra S215HD	Kässbohrer Tornado	C47F	1992	

Operating companies:
Solent Blue Line: 83-97, 149-65, 205-12/24-6/31-5/69/70/5-8/80-2, 402-30, 694/7-709, 721/2/8-34, 817
Southern Vectis: Remainder

Previous Registrations:
390CDL	C316TDL	CXI5971	WJM811T	VDL613S	UFX855S
473CDL	C315TDL	LXI4409	RDL307X	WDL142	WDL310Y
934BDL	A780WHB	TDL998	TDL998, ABK832A	WDL748	C314TDL
A295FDL	A701DDL, WDL142	VDL263	C317TDL	WXI6291	XDL432T

Special Liveries:
Overall Advertisements: 83/5/9, 96, 155/7, 406/16/19, 501/4, 679/83/91/3
Tilling: 301, 563/6/73, 611/28, 806/63.

Named vehicles:
89 *Nick Girdler*, 149 *Southampton Mencap*, 150 *Wendy Knight*, 154 *T S Astrid*, 155 *Josie Nicholls*, 160 *Eileen Howlett*, 161 *British Diabetic Assn, Southampton*, 162 *RSPCA, Action for Animals*, 163 *Romsey Lions*, 164 *Mary Hill*, 721 *Southampton - le Havre Twinning Society*, 864 *Shanklins Pony*.

116

STAGECOACH SOUTH Fleet List

21-26 — Iveco Daily 49.10 — Robin Hood — B23F — 1989

21	F21PSL	22	F22PSL	23	F23PSL	25	F25PSL	26	F26PSL

30	G30PSR	Iveco Daily 49.10	Phoenix	B23F	1989	✓
33	F62AVV	Iveco Daily 49.10	Robin Hood	B23F	1989	

36-43 — Iveco Daily 49.10 — Phoenix — B23F — 1989

36	G36SSR	38	G38SSR	39	G39SSR	42	G42SSR	43	G43SSR
37	G37SSR								

63	E233RJF	Iveco Daily 49.10	Robin Hood	B25F	1987

68	C818SDY	Mercedes-Benz L608D	Alexander AM	B20F	1986
69	C819SDY	Mercedes-Benz L608D	Alexander AM	B20F	1986
70	C820SDY	Mercedes-Benz L608D	Alexander AM	B20F	1986

71-80 — Mercedes-Benz 709D — Alexander AM — B23F* — 1990 — *71-3 are B25F

71	G71APO	73	G73APO	75	G975ARV	77	G977ARV	79	H679BTP
72	G72APO	74	G974ARV	76	G976ARV	78	G978ARV	80	H680BTP

100-118 — Leyland National 11351A/1R — B52F — 1979

100	AYJ100T	104	AYJ104T	110	ENJ910V	113	ENJ913V	116	ENJ916V
101	AYJ101T	105	AYJ105T	111	ENJ911V	114	ENJ914V	117	ENJ917V
102	AYJ102T	107	AYJ107T	112	ENJ912V	115	ENJ915V	118	ENJ918V
103	AYJ103T	109	ENJ909V					

119-126 — Leyland National 2 NL116L11/1R — B52F — 1980

119	GYJ919V	121	GYJ921V	123	HFG923V	125	OUF262W	126	SYC852
120	GYJ920V	122	GYJ922V	124	JNJ194V			

127	FDV830V	Leyland National 2 NL116L11/1R	B52F	1980
128	FDV831V	Leyland National 2 NL116L11/1R	B52F	1980

129-138 — Leyland National 2 NL116AL11/1R — B49F* — 1981 — *129/32 are B45F

129	415DCD	131	411DCD	133	420DCD	135	405DCD	137	407DCD
130	400DCD	132	YLJ332	134	XLD244	136	406DCD	138	410DCD

139	FDV829V	Leyland National 2 NL116L11/1R	B52F	1980	
140	CPO98W	Leyland National 2 NL106L11/1R	B41F	1980	Ex Portsmouth, 1990
141	CPO99W	Leyland National 2 NL106L11/1R	DP40F	1980	Ex Portsmouth, 1990
142	CPO100W	Leyland National 2 NL106L11/1R	DP40F	1980	Ex Portsmouth, 1990
143	ERV115W	Leyland National 2 NL106AL11/1R	B41F	1981	Ex Portsmouth, 1990
144	ERV116W	Leyland National 2 NL106AL11/1R	B41F	1981	Ex Portsmouth, 1990
145	ERV117W	Leyland National 2 NL106AL11/1R	B41F	1981	Ex Portsmouth, 1990
146	ERV118W	Leyland National 2 NL106AL11/1R	B41F	1981	Ex Portsmouth, 1990
148	UFG48S	Leyland National 11351A/2R	B52F	1977	
152	VOD625S	Leyland National 11351A/1R	B52F	1978	Ex Devon General, 1987
153	VOD603S	Leyland National 11351A/1R	B52F	1978	Ex Devon General, 1987
154	VOD604S	Leyland National 11351A/1R	B52F	1978	Ex Devon General, 1987
155	VOD605S	Leyland National 11351A/1R	B52F	1978	Ex Devon General, 1987
161	TRN811V	Leyland National 10351B/1R	B44F	1979	Ex Magicbus, 1991
162	PCD82R	Leyland National 11351A/1R	B49F	1977	
163	PCD73R	Leyland National 11351A/1R	B49F	1976	
168	WYJ168S	Leyland National 11351A/2R	B44D	1978	
169	WYJ168S	Leyland National 11351A/2R	B48F	1978	Fitted with a DAF engine

171-177 — Leyland National 11351A/2R — B48F* — 1978 — 171 is B44D, 173 is B52F

171	WYJ171S	173	YCD73T	174	YCD74T	176	YCD76T	177	YCD77T

178	PCD78R	Leyland National 11351A/1R	B49F	1976
179	PCD79R	Leyland National 11351A/1R	B49F	1977

180	PCD80R	Leyland National 11351A/1R		B49F	1977
182	YCD82T	Leyland National 11351A/2R		B48F	1978
187	YCD87T	Leyland National 11351A/2R		B48F	1978

189-198 Leyland National 11351A/1R — B52F 1979

189	AYJ89T	192	AYJ92T	194	AYJ94T	196	AYJ96T	198	AYJ98T
191	AYJ91T	193	AYJ93T	195	AYJ95T	197	AYJ97T		

201-206 Leyland Olympian ON2R56G13Z4 Alexander RL — H51/36F 1989

201	F601MSL	203	F603MSL	204	F604MSL	205	F605MSL	206	F606MSL
202	F602MSL								

207-214 Leyland Olympian ON2R56G13Z4 Alexander RL — HDP51/31F 1989

207	G807RTS	209	G809RTS	211	G211SSL	213	G213SSL	214	G214SSL
208	G808RTS	210	G210SSL	212	G212SSL				

215-219 Leyland Olympian ON2R56G13Z4 Alexander RL — H51/34F 1990

215	H815CBP	216	H816CBP	217	H817CBP	218	H818CBP	219	H819CBP

220	J720GAP	Leyland Olympian ON2R56G13Z4 Alexander RL	DPH47/27F	1991
221	J721GAP	Leyland Olympian ON2R56G13Z4 Alexander RL	DPH47/27F	1991
222	J722GAP	Leyland Olympian ON2R56G13Z4 Alexander RL	DPH47/27F	1991
223	J623GCR	Leyland Olympian ON2R56G13Z4 Alexander RL	H47/30F	1991
224	J624GCR	Leyland Olympian ON2R56G13Z4 Alexander RL	H47/30F	1991

225-234 Leyland Olympian ON2R56G13Z4 Alexander RL — H51/34F 1990

225	G705TCD	227	G707TCD	229	G709TCD	231	G701TCD	233	G703TCD
226	G706TCD	228	G708TCD	230	G710TCD	232	G702TCD	234	G704TCD

235-240 Leyland Olympian ON2R56G13Z4 Alexander RL — H51/34F 1992

235	K235NHC	237	K237NHC	238	K238NHC	239	K239NHC	240	K240NHC
236	K236NHC								

251-258 Bristol VRT/SL3/6LXB — Eastern Coach Works — H43/31F* 1980 — *251 is DPH43/31F

251	JWV251W	253	JWV253W	255	JWV255W	256	JWV256W	258	JWV258W
252	JWV252W	254	JWV254W						

259	DBV29W	Bristol VRT/SL3/6LXB	Eastern Coach Works	DPH43/31F	1980	Ex Ribble, 1986
265	DBV25W	Bristol VRT/SL3/6LXB	Eastern Coach Works	DPH43/31F	1980	Ex Ribble, 1986

266-276 Bristol VRT/SL3/680 — Eastern Coach Works — H43/31F* 1981 — *266-9 are DPH43/31F / 266-8/76 Gardner engined

266	JWV266W	268	JWV268W	274	JWV274W	275	JWV275W	276	JWV976W
267	JWV267W	269	JWV269W						

301-309 Volvo Citybus B10M-50 — Northern Counties — DPH43/33F 1989

301	F301MYJ	303	F303MYJ	305	F305MYJ	307	F307MYJ	309	F309MYJ
302	F302MYJ	304	F304MYJ	306	F306MYJ	308	F308MYJ		

315	GLJ467N	Bristol VRT/SL2/6LX	Eastern Coach Works	H43/31F	1974	
337	LHG437T	Bristol VRT/SL3/501	Eastern Coach Works	H43/31F	1978	Ex Ribble, 1986
344	XAP644S	Bristol VRT/SL3/6LXB	Eastern Coach Works	H43/31F	1978	
381	UWV611S	Bristol VRT/SL3/6LXB	Eastern Coach Works	CO43/31F	1978	
384	UWV604S	Bristol VRT/SL3/6LXB	Eastern Coach Works	CO43/31F	1977	

387-397 Bristol VRT/SL3/6LXB — Eastern Coach Works — H43/31F 1978

387	VPR486S	391	VPR490S	393	VPR492S	395	YEL2T	397	YEL4T
388	VPR487S	392	VPR491S	394	HFG193T	396	YEL3T		

407	PVT207L	Bristol RESL6L	Eastern Coach Works	B44F	1972	Ex Northern, North Anston, 1989
409	409DCD	Leyland Titan PD3/4	Northern Counties	FCO39/30F	1964	

420-450 — Bristol VRT/SL3/6LXB — Eastern Coach Works — H43/31F — 1979-80

420	ELJ212V	435	FDV839V	440	KRU840W	444	KRU844V	448	LFJ870W
422	FDV818V	438	KRU838W	441	KRU841W	446	LFJ874W	449	LFJ875W
433	FDV834V	439	KRU839W	442	KRU842W	447	LFJ881W	450	LFJ880W

466	OCK366K	Bristol RESL6L	Eastern Coach Works	B47F	1972	Ex Ribble, 1986

501-580 — Dennis Dart 9.8SDL3017 — Alexander Dash — B41F — 1992 — 535-80 are B40F

501	J501GCD	517	J517GCD	533	J533GCD	549	J549GCD	565	K565NHC
502	J502GCD	518	J518GCD	534	J534GCD	550	J550GCD	566	K566NHC
503	J503GCD	519	J519GCD	535	J535GCD	551	J551GCD	567	K567NHC
504	J504GCD	520	J520GCD	536	J536GCD	552	J552GCD	568	K568NHC
505	J505GCD	521	J521GCD	537	J537GCD	553	K553NHC	569	K569NHC
506	J506GCD	522	J522GCD	538	J538GCD	554	K554NHC	570	K570NHC
507	J507GCD	523	J523GCD	539	J539GCD	555	K655NHC	571	K571NHC
508	J508GCD	524	J524GCD	540	J540GCD	556	K556NHC	572	K572NHC
509	J509GCD	525	J525GCD	541	J541GCD	557	K557NHC	573	K573NHC
510	J510GCD	526	J526GCD	542	J542GCD	558	K558NHC	574	K574NHC
511	J511GCD	527	J527GCD	543	J543GCD	559	K559NHC	575	K575NHC
512	J512GCD	528	J528GCD	544	J544GCD	560	K660NHC	576	K576NHC
513	J513GCD	529	J529GCD	545	J545GCD	561	K561NHC	577	K577NHC
514	J514GCD	530	J530GCD	546	J546GCD	562	K562NHC	578	K578NHC
515	J515GCD	531	J531GCD	547	J547GCD	563	K563NHC	579	K579NHC
516	J516GCD	532	J532GCD	548	J548GCD	564	K564NHC	580	K580NHC

607-623 — Bristol VRT/SL3/6LXB — Eastern Coach Works — CO43/31F — 1977-78

607	UWV607S	614	UWV614S	617	UWV617S	621	UWV621S	623	UWV623S

624	NEL124P	Leyland National 11351A/1R		B49F	1976	
636	XAP636S	Bristol VRT/SL3/6LXB	Eastern Coach Works	H43/31F	1978	
647	AAP647T	Bristol VRT/SL3/6LXB	Eastern Coach Works	H43/31F	1978	
648	AAP648T	Bristol VRT/SL3/6LXB	Eastern Coach Works	H43/31F	1978	
649	AAP649T	Bristol VRT/SL3/6LXB	Eastern Coach Works	H43/31F	1978	
658	LHG438T	Bristol VRT/SL3/501	Eastern Coach Works	H43/31F	1978	Ex Ribble, 1986
660	AAP660T	Bristol VRT/SL3/6LXB	Eastern Coach Works	H43/28F	1978	
661	MLJ917P	Leyland National 11351/1R		B49F	1976	
662	AAP660T	Bristol VRT/SL3/6LXB	Eastern Coach Works	H43/28F	1978	
663	PJT263R	Leyland National 11351A/1R		B49F	1976	
666	MLJ922P	Leyland National 11351/1R		B49F	1976	
668	AAP668T	Bristol VRT/SL3/6LXB	Eastern Coach Works	H43/28F	1979	
670	AAP670T	Bristol VRT/SL3/6LXB	Eastern Coach Works	H43/28F	1979	
671	AAP671T	Bristol VRT/SL3/6LXB	Eastern Coach Works	H43/28F	1979	

673-692 — Bristol VRT/SL3/6LXB — Eastern Coach Works — H43/31F — 1979-80

673	EAP973V	680	EAP980V	684	EAP984V	687	EAP987V	691	EAP991V
677	EAP977V	682	EAP982V	685	EAP985V	688	EAP988V	692	EAP992V
678	EAP978V	683	EAP983V	686	EAP986V	690	EAP990V		

693	ELJ213V	Bristol VRT/SL3/6LXB	Eastern Coach Works	H43/31F	1979	
696	EAP996V	Bristol VRT/SL3/6LXB	Eastern Coach Works	H43/31F	1980	
698	RJT146R	Leyland National 11351A/1R		B49F	1977	
703	KKM103P	Bristol VRT/SL3/6LX	Eastern Coach Works	H43/34F	1975	Ex Maidstone & District, 1983
710	UFX851S	Leyland National 11351A/1R		B49F	1977	
712	UFX853S	Leyland National 11351A/1R		B49F	1977	
717	PKM117R	Bristol VRT/SL3/6LXB	Eastern Coach Works	H43/31F	1977	Ex Maidstone & District, 1983
718	VFX984S	Leyland National 11351A/1R		B49F	1978	
724	TEL490R	Leyland National 11351A/1R		DP48F	1977	
726	RHC726S	Leyland Atlantean AN68A/1R	East Lancashire	H43/31F	1978	Ex Eastbourne, 1989
727	RHC727S	Leyland Atlantean AN68A/1R	East Lancashire	H43/31F	1978	Ex Eastbourne, 1989
729	WKO129S	Bristol VRT/SL3/6LXB	Eastern Coach Works	H43/31F	1978	Ex Maidstone & District, 1983
730	WKO129S	Bristol VRT/SL3/6LXB	Eastern Coach Works	H43/31F	1978	Ex Maidstone & District, 1983
731	WFX256S	Leyland National 11351A/1R		DP48F	1978	
734	WPR151S	Leyland National 11351A/1R		B49F	1978	

No.	Reg	Chassis	Body	Layout	Year	Notes
737	VKE565S	Leyland National 11351A/1R		B49F	1977	
741	DRU6T	Leyland National 11351A/1R		B49F	1978	
746	FPR62V	Leyland National 11351A/1R		B49F	1980	
749	BKE849T	Bristol VRT/SL3/6LXB	Eastern Coach Works	H43/31F	1979	Ex Maidstone & District, 1983
750	BKE850T	Bristol VRT/SL3/6LXB	Eastern Coach Works	H43/31F	1979	Ex Maidstone & District, 1983
751	BKE851T	Bristol VRT/SL3/6LXB	Eastern Coach Works	H43/31F	1979	Ex Maidstone & District, 1983
757	UHG757R	Leyland National 11351A/1R		B49F	1977	Ex Ribble, 1986
758	BKE858T	Bristol VRT/SL3/6LXB	Eastern Coach Works	H43/31F	1979	Ex Maidstone & District, 1983
759	BKE859T	Bristol VRT/SL3/6LXB	Eastern Coach Works	H43/31F	1979	Ex Maidstone & District, 1983
760	BKE860T	Bristol VRT/SL3/6LXB	Eastern Coach Works	H43/31F	1979	Ex Maidstone & District, 1983
761	RJT151R	Bristol VRT/SL3/6LXB	Eastern Coach Works	H43/31F	1977	
762	BKE862T	Bristol VRT/SL3/6LXB	Eastern Coach Works	H43/34F	1979	Ex Maidstone & District, 1983
768	CBV768S	Leyland National 11351A/1R		B49F	1978	Ex Ribble, 1986
770	HKE690L	Bristol VRT/SL2/6LX	Eastern Coach Works	O43/34F	1973	Ex Maidstone & District, 1983
771	OWE271K	Bristol VRT/SL2/6LXB	East Lancashire	H43/30F	1972	Ex Maidstone & District, 1983
776	CBV776S	Leyland National 11351A/1R		B49F	1978	Ex Ribble, 1986
784	CBV784S	Leyland National 11351A/1R		B49F	1978	Ex Ribble, 1986
798	CBV798S	Leyland National 11351A/1R		B49F	1978	Ex Ribble, 1986

799-831

Mercedes-Benz L608D — Alexander AM — B20F — 1986

No.	Reg	No.	Reg	No.	Reg	No.	Reg	No.	Reg
799	C799SDY	804	C804SDY	810	C810SDY	815	C815SDY	828	D228UHC
800	C800SDY	807	C807SDY	811	C811SDY	816	C816SDY	830	D230UHC
801	C801SDY	808	C808SDY	813	C813SDY	825	D225UHC	831	D231UHC
803	C803SDY	809	C809SDY	814	C814SDY				

847-852

Mercedes-Benz L608D — Alexander AM — DP19F — 1986

No.	Reg	No.	Reg	No.	Reg	No.	Reg	No.	Reg
847	D947UDY	849	D949UDY	850	D950UDY	851	D951UDY	852	D952UDY
848	D948UDY								

No.	Reg	Chassis	Body	Layout	Year	Notes
891	G91VMM	Leyland Swift LBM6T/2RA	Wadham Stringer Vanguard	B34FL	1990	On loan from East Sussex CC
892	G92VMM	Leyland Swift LBM6T/2RA	Wadham Stringer Vanguard	B34FL	1990	On loan from East Sussex CC
901	F561HPP	MCW MetroRider MF158/9	MCW	B33F	1988	Ex Chatfield, Worthing, 1989
902	F562HPP	MCW MetroRider MF158/9	MCW	B33F	1988	Ex Chatfield, Worthing, 1989
903	F563HPP	MCW MetroRider MF158/9	MCW	B33F	1988	Ex Chatfield, Worthing, 1989
904	F564HPP	MCW MetroRider MF158/9	MCW	B33F	1988	Ex Chatfield, Worthing, 1989
905	419DCD	MCW MetroRider MF158/9	MCW	DP28F	1988	Ex Chatfield, Worthing, 1989
906	416DCD	MCW MetroRider MF158/10	MCW	B31F	1988	Ex East Midland, 1989
907	417DCD	MCW MetroRider MF154/1	MCW	B31F	1988	Ex East Midland, 1989
908	418DCD	MCW MetroRider MF158/3	MCW	DP33F	1988	Ex East Midland, 1989

911-916

Mercedes-Benz L608D — PMT — B20F — 1986

No.	Reg	No.	Reg	No.	Reg	No.	Reg	No.	Reg
911	C591SHC	913	C593SHC	914	C594SHC	915	C595SHC	916	C596SHC

918-922

Iveco Daily 49.10 — Phoenix — B23F — 1989

No.	Reg	No.	Reg	No.	Reg	No.	Reg	No.	Reg
918	G418RYJ	919	G419RYJ	920	G420RYJ	921	G421RYJ	922	G422RYJ

No.	Reg	Chassis	Body	Layout	Year	Notes
925	E65BVS	Iveco Daily 49.10	Robin Hood	B25F	1988	
931	G34PSR	Iveco Daily 49.10	Phoenix	B23F	1989	
946	MFN946F	AEC Regent V 3D3RA	Park Royal	H40/32F	1967	Ex East Kent, 1983
955	D935EBP	Iveco Daily 49.10	Robin Hood	B19F	1987	
961	F61AVV	Iveco Daily 49.10	Robin Hood	B25F	1989	
1001	401DCD	Leyland Tiger TRCTL11/2R	Plaxton Paramount 3200	C50F	1983	
1002	402DCD	Leyland Tiger TRCTL11/2R	Plaxton Paramount 3200	C50F	1983	
1003	403DCD	Leyland Tiger TRCTL11/3R	Plaxton Paramount 3200	C50F	1983	
1004	BYJ919Y	Leyland Tiger TRCTL11/3R	Plaxton Paramount 3200	C50F	1983	
1005	UWP105	Leyland Tiger TRCTL11/3R	Plaxton Paramount 3200	C50F	1983	
1006	896HOD	Volvo B10M-61	Plaxton Paramount 3500 II	C40FT	1985	
1007	495FFJ	Volvo B10M-61	Plaxton Paramount 3500 II	C50F	1985	
1066	MSU466	Leyland Tiger TRCTL11/3RH	Duple 340	C53FT	1987	Ex Fife Scottish, 1991
1167	NFX667	Leyland Leopard PSU5E/4R	Plaxton Supreme V	C50F	1982	
1170	ELJ208V	Leyland Leopard PSU3E/4R	Plaxton Supreme Exp	C53F	1979	
1171	VSV564	Leyland Tiger TRCTL11/3R	Plaxton Paramount 3200 E	C49F	1983	Ex Maidstone & District, 1985
1172	USV672	Leyland Tiger TRCTL11/3R	Plaxton Paramount 3200 E	C49F	1983	Ex Maidstone & District, 1985
1193	YEL93Y	Leyland Leopard PSU5E/4R	Eastern Coach Works B51	C52F	1982	
1194	YEL94Y	Leyland Leopard PSU5E/4R	Eastern Coach Works B51	C55F	1982	

1358	408DCD	Leyland Leopard PSU5D/4R	Plaxton Paramount 3200 (1984) C53F		1981
1362	412DCD	Leyland Leopard PSU5E/4R	Plaxton Supreme V	C50F	1982
1364	413DCD	Leyland Leopard PSU5E/4R	Plaxton Supreme V	C50F	1982
3223	424DCD	Leyland Titan PD3/4	Northern Counties	FO39/30F	1964

Operating Companies:

Coastline Buses: 100/19-40/52/68/71/89/91/2/8, 209/22-4/31-4/51/3-6/8/9/65-9/74-6, 304-9, 541-52, 607/14/7/36/47-9/62/70/1/7/8/80/2-7/90-2/6, 757/68/98, 901-4/6/8/18-22/5/31, 955/61, 3223

Hampshire Bus: 21-3/5/6, 30/3/6-9, 42/3, 63/8-80, 201-8/10-9/25-30, 315/37/44/81/4/7/8/91-7, 420/2/33/5, 438-42/4/6-50, 522-40, 624/61/3/6/98, 710/2/8/24/31/4/5/41/6/76/84, 905/7, 1003-7, 1167/70/93.

Hastings Buses: 141-6/61, 407/66, 501-20, 658/93, 703/17/26/7/9/30/49-51/8-62/70/1, 816/25/8/30/1/47-52, 946, 1001/2/66, 1171/2, 1358/62/4.

Southdown Buses: 101-5/7/9-18/48/9/53-5/62/3/9/73/4/6-80/2/7/93-7, 220/1/52, 301-3, 409, 521, 621/3/60/8/73/88, 799-801/3/4/7-11/3-5/91/2, 911/3-6, 1194.

Previous Registrations:

400DCD	RUF430X		413DCD	HHC364Y	JNJ194V	HFG924V, DSV943
401DCD	XUF531Y		415DCD	RUF429X	MSU466	D526ESG
402DCD	XUF532Y, 2880CD		416DCD	F816CWJ	NFX667	HHC367Y
403DCD	XUF533Y		417DCD	F817DWG	OUF262W	JWV125, LYJ145
405DCD	RUF435X		418DCD	E518YWF	SYC852	JWV126W
406DCD	RUF436X		419DCD	F565HPP	USV672	FKL172Y
407DCD	RUF437X		420DCD	RUF433X, MSV533	UWP105	XUF535Y
408DCD	LPN358W		424DCD	424DCD, AOR158B	VSV564	FKL171Y
410DCD	RUF438X		495FFJ	B193CGA	XLD244	RUF434X
411DCD	RUF431X		896HOD	B192CGA	YLJ332	RUF432X
412DCD	TFG222X	BYJ919Y		XUF534Y, 404DCD		

Special Liveries:

National Express: 1066, 1358
Overall Advertisements: 43, 129/32, 267/74, 512, 617/47/82-4, 734/46.

THAMES TRANSIT GROUP Fleet List

1	AOD648Y	Leyland Tiger TRCTL11/3R	Plaxton Paramount 3200	C46FT	1983	Ex Devon General, 1987
2	AOD649Y	Leyland Tiger TRCTL11/3R	Plaxton Paramount 3200	C46FT	1983	Ex Devon General, 1987
3	B400UOD	Leyland Tiger TRCTL11/3RH	Duple Laser 2	C44FT	1985	Ex Devon General, 1987
4	B401UOD	Leyland Tiger TRCTL11/3RH	Duple Laser 2	C44FT	1985	Ex Devon General, 1987
5	B402UOD	Leyland Tiger TRCTL11/3RH	Duple Laser 2	C44FT	1985	Ex Devon General, 1987
7	B405UOD	Leyland Tiger TRCTL11/3RH	Duple Laser 2	C42FT	1985	Ex Devon General, 1987
9	D142PTT	Leyland Tiger TRCTL11/3RH	Plaxton Paramount 3500 III	C51F	1987	
10	PYV277	Leyland Tiger TRCTL11/3RZ	Plaxton Paramount 3500 II	C51F	1986	Ex Devon General, 1987
11	LSV670	Leyland Tiger TRCTL11/3RZ	Plaxton Paramount 3500 II	C51F	1986	Ex Devon General, 1987
14	B404UOD	Leyland Tiger TRCTL11/3RH	Duple Laser 2	C44FT	1985	Ex Devon General, 1988
15	C922HYA	Leyland Tiger TRCTL11/3RZ	Plaxton Paramount 3200 II	C49FT	1986	Ex Southern National, 1989
16	B896YYD	Leyland Tiger TRCTL11/3RH	Plaxton Paramount 3500	C48FT	1985	Ex Devon General, 1990
17	B894YYD	Leyland Tiger TRCTL11/3RH	Plaxton Paramount 3500	C48FT	1985	Ex Devon General, 1990
18	H69CFJ	Volvo B10M-60	Plaxton Paramount 3200 III	C53FT	1990	

19-23

		Volvo B10M-60	Ikarus Blue Danube	C49FT	1991

19	H913FTT	20	H914FTT	21	H915FTT	22	H916FTT	23	H917FTT

24	J499MOD	Volvo B10M-60	Ikarus Blue Danube	C49FT	1992	
97	AFJ741T	Bristol LH6L	Plaxton Supreme III Exp	C41F	1979	Ex Devon General, 1987

100-141 — Ford Transit VE6 — Mellor — B16F — 1986-87

100	D100PTT	109	D109PTT	118	D118PTT	126	D126PTT	134	D134PTT
101	D101PTT	110	D110PTT	119	D119PTT	127	D127PTT	135	D135PTT
102	D102PTT	111	D111PTT	120	D120PTT	128	D128PTT	136	D136PTT
103	D103PTT	112	D112PTT	121	D121PTT	129	D129PTT	137	D137PTT
104	D104PTT	113	D113PTT	122	D122PTT	130	D130PTT	138	D138PTT
105	D105PTT	114	D114PTT	123	D123PTT	131	D131PTT	139	D139PTT
106	D106PTT	115	D115PTT	124	D124PTT	132	D132PTT	140	D140PTT
107	D107PTT	116	D116PTT	125	D125PTT	133	D133PTT	141	D776NDV
108	D108PTT	117	D117PTT						

142	E825ATT	Ford Transit VE6	Mellor	B16F	1988	Ex Docklands Transit, 1990
143	E826ATT	Ford Transit VE6	Mellor	B16F	1988	Ex Docklands Transit, 1990
144	E827ATT	Ford Transit VE6	Mellor	B16F	1988	Ex Docklands Transit, 1990
145	E828ATT	Ford Transit VE6	Mellor	B16F	1988	Ex Docklands Transit, 1990

200-222 — Ford Transit VE6 — Mellor — B16F — 1987-88

200	E200BDV	205	E205BDV	210	E210BDV	215	E215BDV	219	E219BDV
201	E201BDV	206	E206BDV	211	E211BDV	216	E216BDV	220	E220BDV
202	E202BDV	207	E207BDV	212	E212BDV	217	E217BDV	221	E221BDV
203	E203BDV	208	E208BDV	213	E213BDV	218	E218BDV	222	E222BDV
204	E204BDV	209	E209BDV	214	E214BDV				

250-259 — Ford Transit VE6 — Mellor — B16F — 1988-88

250	F750FDV	252	F752FDV	254	F754FDV	256	E196BDV	258	E198BDV
251	F751FDV	253	F753FDV	255	F755FDV	257	E197BDV	259	E199BDV

287	XTP287L	Leyland Atlantean AN68/1R	Alexander AL	H45/30D	1973

300-324 — Mercedes-Benz 709D — Reeve Burgess Beaver — DP25F — 1988 — Ex South Midland, 1988

300	E300BWL	305	E305BWL	310	F310EJO	315	F315EJO	320	F320EJO
301	E301BWL	306	E306BWL	311	F311EJO	316	F316EJO	321	F321EJO
302	E302BWL	307	E307BWL	312	F312EJO	317	F317EJO	322	F322EJO
303	E303BWL	308	E308BWL	313	F313EJO	318	F318EJO	323	F323EJO
304	E304BWL	309	E309BWL	314	F314EJO	319	F319EJO	324	F324EJO

325-346 — Mercedes-Benz 709D — Reeve Burgess Beaver — B25F — 1989

325	F775FDV	330	F767FDV	335	F405KOD	339	F409KOD	343	F413KOD
326	F776FDV	331	F768FDV	336	F406KOD	340	F410KOD	344	F402KOD
327	F764FDV	332	F769FDV	337	F407KOD	341	F411KOD	345	F403KOD
328	F765FDV	333	F770FDV	338	F408KOD	342	F412KOD	346	F746FDV
329	F766FDV	334	F404KOD						

347-354 — Mercedes-Benz 709D — Carlyle — B29F — 1990

347	G947TDV	349	G949TDV	351	G951TDV	353	G953TDV	354	G954TDV
348	G948TDV	350	G950TDV	352	G952TDV				

367-409 — Mercedes-Benz 811D — Carlyle — B29F — 1991

367	H985FTT	376	H994FTT	385	H176GTA	394	H785GTA	402	H103HDV
368	H986FTT	377	H995FTT	386	H177GTA	395	H786GTA	403	H104HDV
369	H987FTT	378	H996FTT	387	H178GTA	396	H787GTA	404	H105HDV
370	H988FTT	379	H997FTT	388	H179GTA	397	H788GTA	405	H106HDV
371	H989FTT	380	H171GTA	389	H180GTA	398	H789GTA	406	H107HDV
372	H990FTT	381	H172GTA	390	H781GTA	399	H790GTA	407	H108HDV
373	H991FTT	382	H173GTA	391	H782GTA	400	H101HDV	408	H109HDV
374	H992FTT	383	H174GTA	392	H783GTA	401	H102HDV	409	H110HDV
375	H993FTT	384	H175GTA	393	H784GTA				

636-656 — Ford Transit 190D — Mellor — B16F — 1987

636	D636NOD	641	D641NOD	645	D645NOD	649	D649NOD	653	D653NOD
637	D637NOD	642	D642NOD	646	D646NOD	650	D650NOD	654	D654NOD
638	D638NOD	643	D643NOD	647	D647NOD	651	D651NOD	655	D655NOD
639	D639NOD	644	D644NOD	648	D648NOD	652	D652NOD	656	D656NOD
640	D640NOD								

780-824

780-824		Ford Transit VE6		Mellor		B16F	1987-88 824 ex Devon General, 1991	

780	D780NDV	791	D791NDV	803	E803WDV	815	E815WDV	822	E822WDV
782	D782NDV	793	D793NDV	806	E806WDV	817	E817WDV	823	E823WDV
783	D783NDV	798	D798NDV	807	E807WDV	820	E820WDV	824	E824WDV

771-821

| **771-821** | | Ford Transit VE6 | | Mellor | | B16F | 1987-88 | |

771	F771FDV	784	D784NDV	794	D794NDV	802	E802WDV	812	E812WDV
772	F772FDV	785	D785NDV	795	D795NDV	804	E804WDV	813	E813WDV
773	F773FDV	786	D786NDV	796	D796NDV	805	E805WDV	814	E814WDV
775	D775NDV	787	D787NDV	797	D797NDV	808	E808WDV	816	E816WDV
777	D777NDV	788	D788NDV	799	D799NDV	809	E809WDV	818	E818WDV
778	D778NDV	789	D789NDV	800	E800WDV	810	E810WDV	819	E819WDV
779	D779NDV	790	D790NDV	801	E801WDV	811	E811WDV	821	E821WDV
781	D781NDV	792	D792NDV						

921	VUD29X	Leyland Leopard PSU3G/4R	Eastern Coach Works B51	C49F	1982	Ex South Midland, 1988
924	EYH808V	Leyland Leopard PSU3E/4R	Duple Dominant II	C49F	1980	Ex South Midland, 1988
925	EYH810V	Leyland Leopard PSU3E/4R	Duple Dominant II	C49F	1980	Ex South Midland, 1988
955	F24PSL	Iveco Daily 49.10	Robin Hood	B23F	1989	
956	D618BCK	Iveco Daily 49.10	Robin Hood	B21F	1987	
957	D939ECR	Iveco Daily 49.10	Robin Hood	B19F	1986	
958	D937ECR	Iveco Daily 49.10	Robin Hood	B19F	1986	

959-973

| **959-973** | | Iveco Daily 49.10 | | Robin Hood | | B23F | 1988 | |

959	E959LPX	962	E962LPX	965	E965LPX	968	E968LPX	971	E971LPX
960	E960LPX	963	E963LPX	966	E966LPX	969	E969LPX	972	E972LPX
961	E961LPX	964	E964LPX	967	E967LPX	970	E970LPX	973	E973LPX

995-999

| **995-999** | | Leyland Tiger TRBTL11/2RP | | Plaxton Derwent | | B54F | 1988 | Ex Burtons, Brixham, 1989-90 | |

995	F278HOD	996	F279HOD	997	F280HOD	998	F281HOD	999	F282HOD

1000	LRV992	Leyland Titan PD2/12	Metro-Cammell	O33/26R	1956	Ex Southdown, 1991
1006	A474NJK	Leyland Tiger TRCTL11/3R	Duple Laser	C50F	1984	Ex Southdown, 1991

Previous Registrations:
A474NJK   A806CCD, 416DCD   LSV670   C129KJO   PYY277   C128KJO

Named vehicles: 3 *Trinity*, 4 *Brasenose*, 7 *St Peters*, 9 *Magdalen*, 10 *Oriel*, 11 *Queens*, 14 *Balliol*, 15 *St Catherine's*.

Operating Units:
Blue Admiral fleet: 101/2/5/19/25/31/41, 200/2/4-22/50-5/7-9, 286, 636-42/4/6-51/3/6, 771-821, 1000
Red Admiral fleet: 106, 201/3/56, 367-409, 643/5, 780/2/3/91/3/8, 803/6/7/15/7/20/2-4, 955-73.

AUTOPOINT Fleet List

4058AP	Ford R1014	Duple Dominant	C45F	1974	Ex Jackson, Eastbourne, 1987
5752AP	Bedford YMT	Duple Dominant	C53F	1976	Ex Leamland, Hassocks, 1986
5501AP	Bedford YMT	Van Hool-McArdle	C53F	1978	Ex Day & Butland, Westham, 1987
3069AP	Ford R1014	Plaxton Supreme IV	C45F	1978	Ex London Borough of Barking, 1988
9925AP	Ford R1114	Duple Dominant II	C53F	1978	Ex Shrubb & Howard, Tatsfield, 1989
5536AP	Bristol LHS6L	Plaxton Supreme III	C33F	1979	Ex Hazeldine, Bilston, 1988
3442AP	Leyland Leopard PSU3E/4R	Van Hool Aragon	C53F	1979	Ex Horlock, Northfleet, 1987
7693AP	Mercedes-Benz L508D	Robin Hood	C18F	1980	Ex Plumpton Coaches, 1990
1241AP	Mercedes-Benz L508D	Reeve Burgess	C21F	1982	Ex Michael's, Carshalton, 1985
FNM739Y	Ford A0610	Mellor	B24F	1983	Ex Ash, Leatherhead, 1986
DBJ371Y	Ford Transit 190	Steedrive	B16F	1983	Ex Upper Waveney , 1986
8903AP	Volvo B10M-61	Van Hool Alizée H	C49FT	1983	Ex Shearings, 1989
9415AP	Mercedes-Benz L207D	Coachcraft	C12F	1983	Ex Michaels, Croydon, 1986
2779AP	Mercedes-Benz L608D	Robin Hood	C25F	1984	Ex Purley Car, Warlingham, 1984
7634AP	Mercedes-Benz L608D	Robin Hood	C21F	1986	
2317AP	Mercedes-Benz L608D	PMT	B20F	1986	Ex Southdown, 1991
C592SHC	Mercedes-Benz L608D	PMT	B20F	1986	Ex Southdown, 1991

9163AP	Bedford YMPS	Plaxton Paramount 3200 III	C33F	1987	
D759TTU	Mercedes-Benz 709D	Advanced Vehicle Bodies	C25F	1987	
D907MVU	Freight Rover Sherpa 350	Made-to-Measure	B16F	1987	Ex Khan, Crawley, 1987
E863UKO	Ford Transit VE6	Dormobile	B20F	1987	Ex Ford demonstrator, 1991
F361JYJ	Mercedes-Benz 609D	Reeve Burgess Beaver	DP19F	1988	
1509AP	Mercedes-Benz 609D	North West Coach Sales	DP24F	1989	

Previous Registrations:

1241AP	OML730X	4058AP	GBM765N	8903AP	ENF578Y, SPR124, GNF470Y
1509AP	F255KDM	5501AP	BUR428T		
2317AP	C590SHC	5536AP	CTM415T	9163AP	D39WDY
2779AP	A311STR	5752AP	MPE773P	9415AP	A605TGO
3069AP	WMM100T	7634AP	C204BCR	9925AP	UME389S
3442AP	CTM417T	7693AP	KFG956W		

BEXHILL BUS CO Fleet List

24	A904MHC	Bedford YNT	Plaxton Paramount 3200	C53F	1984	
410	MVT210K	Bristol RELH6L	Eastern Coach Works	B49F	1972	Ex Hastings Buses, 1990
412	AHT212J	Bristol RELL6L	Eastern Coach Works	B50F	1971	Ex Hastings Buses, 1990
416	HHW916L	Bristol RELL6L	Eastern Coach Works	B50F	1972	Ex Hastings Buses, 1990
417	NLJ517M	Bristol LH6L	Eastern Coach Works	B43F	1973	Ex Manxtree, Bexhill, 1984
423	PVT223L	Bristol RELL6L	Eastern Coach Works	B53F	1973	Ex Hastings Buses, 1990
428	PVT228L	Bristol RELL6L	Eastern Coach Works	B53F	1973	Ex Hastings Buses, 1990
442	PLJ742G	Bristol RELL6G	Eastern Coach Works	B45D	1969	Ex Purnell, Harold Hill, 1989

	NDY269R	Bedford YMT	Duple Dominant I	C53F	1976	
	UMJ452W	Bedford YMQS	Plaxton Supreme IV	C35F	1981	
	GPX585X	Mercedes-Benz L508D	Robin Hood	DP19F	1982	Ex Transcity, Sidcup, 1990
	HEW312Y	Mercedes-Benz L508D	Reeve Burgess	C19F	1983	
	A844UGB	Volvo B10M-61	Van Hool Alizée H	C49FT	1984	
	A132MBA	Leyland Tiger TRCTL11/3RZ	Plaxton Paramount 3500	C49FT	1984	Ex Boro'line, Maidstone, 1989
	A408GPY	Kässbohrer Setra S228HDT	Kässbohrer Imperial	CH54/20CT	1984	Ex Zebra, Trimdon Grange, 1988
	B88AMH	Leyland Tiger TRCTL11/3R	Van Hool Alizée	C53F	1984	Ex Sault & Roff, London SE15, 1989
	C602PUF	Mercedes-Benz L608D	Reeve Burgess	B16FL	1985	Ex Community Transport, Hove, 1991
	H538CTR	Leyland Swift ST2R44C97A4	Wadham Stringer Vanguard II	B34FL	1990	

BLUE SALOON Fleet List

OFR970M	AEC Swift 3MP2R	Marshall	B47D	1974	Ex Blackpool, 1988
YRO549N	Bristol LHL6L	Plaxton Elite III	C51F	1974	Ex Roots, Puttenham, 1989
KPB881P	Bristol LH6L	Eastern Coach Works	B43F	1975	
KPM429P	Bristol LH6L	Plaxton Supreme III Exp	C45F	1975	
KJD427P	Bristol LH6L	Eastern Coach Works	B39F	1976	Ex Davies, Carmarthen, 1985
TMJ637R	Bristol LHL6L	Plaxton Supreme III	C53F	1976	Ex Crawt, Guildford, 1989
TPJ61S	Bristol LHS6L	Eastern Coach Works	B35F	1977	Ex Hurstwood House School, 1990
VDV107S	Bristol LH6L	Eastern Coach Works	B43F	1978	Ex Devon General, 1985
VRY724S	Bedford YMT	Plaxton Supreme III	C53F	1978	Ex Warner, Milford, 1983
YPH406T	Bedford YMT	Plaxton Supreme IV	C53F	1978	
YPH407T	Bedford YMT	Plaxton Supreme IV	C53F	1978	
YPB820T	Bedford YMT	Plaxton Supreme IV	C53F	1978	
CPD131T	Bristol LH6L	Eastern Coach Works	B43F	1979	
HPB814V	Bedford YMT	Plaxton Supreme IV	C53F	1978	
KPC405W	Bedford YMT	Duple Dominant IV	C53F	1980	Ex Warner, Milford, 1983
WLP958X	Bedford CFS	Dormobile	C12F	1982	Ex Tentrek, Sidcup, 1987
HBH426Y	Leyland Tiger TRCTL11/3R	Plaxton Paramount 3200	C53F	1983	
776WME	Leyland Royal Tiger B54	Roe Doyen	C46FT	1984	
1311VY	Leyland Royal Tiger B50	Van Hool Alizée	C53F	1985	
OYD693	Hestair Duple 425	Duple 425	C53F	1989	

Previous Registrations:
OYD693   G602LKU

Special Liveries:
Hoppa Shoppa: KPB881P, VDV107S, CPD131T

BYGONE BUSES Fleet List

Reg	Chassis	Body	Type	Year	History
HAA874	Bedford OB	Duple Vista	C29F	1949	Ex Taylor, Sutton Scotney, 1988
677DYE	AEC Routemaster	Park Royal	H36/28R	1963	Ex London Buses, 1989
8056UA	Leyland Leopard PSU3B/4R	Willowbrook Crusader (1990)	C48FT	1971	Ex Ranger, London SE25, 1990
AEL105K	Bristol RELL6G	Eastern Coach Works	B45D	1972	Ex Farmer, Ashford, 1992
MLH441L	Daimler Fleetline CRL6	MCW	H44/29F	1973	Ex Hunt, Alford, 1991
XDL794L	Leyland National 1151/1R/0501		B46D	1973	Ex Athelstan, Chippenham, 1990
OAE956M	Bristol RELL6L	Eastern Coach Works	B50F	1973	Ex Westbus, Ashford, 1992
GKL826N	Bristol VRT/SL2/6LX	Eastern Coach Works	H43/34F	1974	Ex Maidstone & District, 1990
NHG732P	Leyland Titan B15/04	Park Royal	H44/32F	1975	Ex Kinch, Barrow-u-Soar, 1991
OKE137P	Leyland Leopard PSU3C/4R	Duple Dominant	C49F	1976	Ex Hastings Buses, 1991
OKE139P	Leyland Leopard PSU3C/4R	Duple Dominant	C47F	1976	Ex Hastings Buses, 1990
1256RU	AEC Reliance 6U3ZR	Plaxton Supreme III	C53F	1976	Ex Nu-Venture, Aylesford, 1991
THX493S	Leyland Fleetline FE30AGR	Park Royal	H44/24D	1977	Ex London Buses, 1992
THX533S	Leyland Fleetline FE30AGR	Park Royal	H44/27D	1978	Ex London Buses, 1992
YWK4S	Bedford YMT	Plaxton Supreme	C53F	1978	Ex Craker, Maidstone, 1991
DFS803S	Seddon Pennine 7	Plaxton Supreme III Express	C49F	1978	Ex Dunn-Line, Notingham, 1992
DFS804S	Seddon Pennine 7	Plaxton Supreme III Express	C49F	1978	Ex Dunn-Line, Notingham, 1992
302TKR	Leyland Leopard PSU5C/4R	Plaxton Viewmaster	C53F	1978	Ex Hollis Coaches, 1992
815BLN	Leyland Leopard PSU5C/4R	Duple Dominant II	C53F	1980	Ex Hastings Buses, 1991

Previous Registrations:

1256RU	KUW523P	8056UA	YDF323K
302TKR	ETU964S, OBF706, VHV83S	815BLN	JKM164V

Named vehicles:
XDL794L *Red Deer*, GKL826N *Red Rooster*, OKE137P *Red Start*, OKE139P *Red Robin*, 815BLN *Red Admiral*.

CHALKWELL COACH HIRE Fleet List

Reg	Chassis	Body	Type	Year	History
KIW6512	Ford R1114	Plaxton Supreme IV	C53F	1980	Ex Dobsons, Widnes, 1984
PNW315W	Ford R1114	Plaxton Supreme IV	C53F	1981	Ex Wallace Arnold, 1986
XPP285X	Leyland Tiger TRCTL11/3R	Plaxton Supreme IV	C57F	1981	Ex Cotterells, Mitcheldean, 1992
TKM108X	Bedford YMT	Wadham Stringer Vanguard	B60F	1982	Ex Happy Days, Woodseaves, 1990
TKM111X	Bedford YMT	Wadham Stringer Vanguard	B60F	1982	Ex Happy Days, Woodseaves, 1990
A438NKL	Talbot Express	Rootes	B14FL	1983	Ex Leybourne Grange Hospital, 1990
KIW6419	Leyland Tiger TRCTL11/2R	Plaxton Paramount 3200 E	C53F	1983	Ex Mainwaring, Gilfach Goch, 1990
KIW7360	Leyland Tiger TRCTL11/2R	Plaxton Paramount 3200	C53F	1984	Ex Mainwaring, Gilfach Goch, 1990
KIW8923	Leyland Tiger TRCTL11/3R	Plaxton Paramount 3200	C53F	1984	Ex Brown, South Kirkby, 1989
KIW8924	Leyland Tiger TRCTL11/3R	Plaxton Paramount 3500	C53F	1984	Ex Elgar & Fox, Inkpen, 1989
A708NGS	Ford Transit 190	Chassis Developments	B12F	1984	Ex Routledge, Cockermouth, 1987
C552DKE	Ford Transit 190	Chassis Developments	C16F	1985	
C147CKL	Mercedes-Benz L307D	Robin Hood	C12F	1985	
C148GGP	Mercedes-Benz L508D	Devon Conversions	C15FL	1985	Ex Kent CC, 1990
D991WDY	Mercedes-Benz 609D	Pilcher-Greene	B16FL	1987	Ex Sochulbus, Ashford, 1990
D658TKX	Ford Transit 130	Chassis Developments	C12F	1987	Ex Dewberry, Biggin Hill, 1988
D575PKW	Ford Transit 130	Coachcraft	C12F	1987	
D339JUM	Volkswagen LT55	Optare City Pacer	DP25F	1988	Ex London Buses, 1992
D345JUM	Volkswagen LT55	Optare City Pacer	DP25F	1988	Ex London Buses, 1992
D354JUM	Volkswagen LT55	Optare City Pacer	DP25F	1988	Ex London Buses, 1992
D355JUM	Volkswagen LT55	Optare City Pacer	DP25F	1988	Ex London Buses, 1992
D360JUM	Volkswagen LT55	Optare City Pacer	DP25F	1988	Ex London Buses, 1992
E26XKP	Mercedes-Benz L307D	Devon Conversions	C12F	1988	
E360KPO	Iveco Daily 49.10	Robin Hood	C25F	1988	Ex Farnham Coaches, 1988
F939KKX	Peugeot-Talbot Express	Chassis Developments	C14F	1988	
F749EKM	Mercedes-Benz L307D	Devon Conversions	C12F	1988	
H847DKL	Mercedes-Benz 814D	Phoenix	C33F	1990	

Previous Registrations:

KIW6512	SMB264V	KIW7360	A234GNR	KIW8924	A152RMJ
KIW6419	A379ROU	KIW8923	A719OWT		

CHILTERN QUEENS Fleet List

Reg	Chassis	Body	Seating	Year	History
ANL807B	AEC Reliance 2MU4RA	Plaxton Panorama	C41F	1964	Ex Liley, Basingstoke, 1977
TUD167G	AEC Reliance 6U3ZR	Plaxton Elite	C57F	1968	
TYD122G	AEC Reliance 6MU3R	Duple	B45F	1968	Ex Tillingbourne, 1980
FPX701H	AEC Reliance 6U3ZR	Plaxton Elite	C51F	1970	Ex Byng, Portsmouth, 1972
OBK602H	AEC Reliance 6MU4RE	Plaxton Elite	C26FT	1970	Ex Byng, Portsmouth, 1972
CYA181J	AEC Reliance 6MU3R	Plaxton Derwent	B47F	1971	Ex Brutonian, Bruton, 1988
ABW777J	AEC Reliance 6U3ZR	Plaxton Elite II	C53F	1971	
EUD256K	AEC Reliance 6MU4R	Plaxton Derwent	B47F	1972	
OJO835M	Leyland Leopard PSU3B/4R	Plaxton Derwent	B55F	1974	
HCS795N	Leyland Leopard PSU3/3R	Alexander AYS	B53F	1975	Ex Clydeside Scottish, 1987
VBW581	Leyland Leopard PSU5A/4R	Plaxton Supreme	C57F	1976	
RFC10T	Leyland Leopard PSU3E/4R	Duple Dominant II Exp	C49F	1978	Ex City of Oxford, 1989
RFC12T	Leyland Leopard PSU3E/4R	Duple Dominant II Exp	C49F	1978	Ex City of Oxford, 1990
WUD815T	Leyland Leopard PSU3E/4R	Duple Dominant II Exp	C49F	1978	Ex City of Oxford, 1990
591STT	Leyland Leopard PSU3E/4R	Plaxton Supreme IV Exp	C53F	1979	
BMO891T	AEC Reliance 6U3ZR	Marshall Camagna	B54F	1979	Ex Ministry of Defence, 1988
YFC18V	Leyland Leopard PSU3E/4R	Duple Dominant II Express	C49F	1979	Ex City of Oxford, 1991
LUA244V	Volvo B58-61	Plaxton Supreme IV	C51F	1980	Ex Parry, Leominster, 1985
PJH582X	Leyland Leopard PSU3E/4R	Plaxton Supreme IV	C53F	1982	
B915CMR	MAN SR280	MAN	C53F	1984	Ex Lee & Back, Caversham, 1991
B911SPR	Volvo B10M-61	Plaxton Paramount 3200 II	C53F	1985	Ex Excelsior, Bournemouth, 1987
C644SJM	Volvo B10M-61	Plaxton Paramount 3200 II	C53F	1986	
D262HFX	Volvo B10M-61	Plaxton Paramount 3200 III	C53F	1987	Ex Excelsior, Bournemouth, 1988
E533PRU	Volvo B10M-61	Plaxton Paramount 3200 III	C48FT	1987	
F986TTF	Mercedes-Benz 811D	Optare StarRider	B33F	1987	Ex Lee & Back, Caversham, 1991
F344TSC	Mercedes-Benz 811D	Alexander AM	DP29F	1987	Ex Challenger, Bridgenorth, 1992
H788RWJ	Scania K93CRB	Plaxton Paramount 3200 III	C55F	1990	

Previous Registrations:

591STT	UUD623T	BMO891T	48AC88	VBW581	SFC2P

COASTAL COACHES Fleet List

No	Reg	Chassis	Seating	Year	History
101	XS2210	Leyland National 10351/1R	DP39F	1976	Ex London Country SW, 1990
102	VY2150	Leyland National 10351A/1R	B41F	1977	Ex East Kent, 1991

Previous Registrations:

VY2150	PJJ343S	XS2210	LPB189P

DONSWAY Fleet List

Reg	Chassis	Body	Seating	Year	History
OUP499M	Bedford YRT	Plaxton Elite Express III	C53F	1973	Ex OK, Bishop Auckland, 1980
HRR757N	Bedford YRT	Plaxton Elite Express III	C53F	1975	Ex Barton, Chiswell, 1982
UJP94S	Bedford YMT	Duple Dominant II	C53F	1978	Ex Eavesway, Ashton-in-Makerfield, 1984
SJK938S	Bedford YMT	Plaxton Supreme III	C49F	1978	Ex Waterhouse, Polegate, 1986
YMJ546S	Bedford YMT	Plaxton Supreme III	C53F	1978	Ex Marinair, Cliftonville, 1987
THX235S	Leyland National 10351A/2R		B36D	1978	Ex London Buses, 1989
NSV130	Leyland Leopard PSU5C/4R	Duple Dominant II	C50F	1979	Ex Shamrock & Rambler, 1988
D344JUM	Volkswagen LT55	Optare City Pacer	B25F	1988	Ex London Buses, 1992

Previous Registrations:

NSV130	AFH196T

Named Vehicles:

OUP499M *Private Enterprise VI*, HRR757N *Private Enterprise IV*, UJP94S *Private Enterprise VII*, SJK938S, *Private Enterprise IX*, YMJ546S *Private Enterprise VI*, NSV130 *Private Enterprise IX*.

EAST SURREY BUSES (Buses) Fleet List

7	OTR411S	Bedford YMT	Duple Dominant	C53F	1977	Ex Coliseum, West End, 1984
8	TAA744T	Bedford YMT	Plaxton	C53F	1979	Ex Taylor, Caterham, 1986
10	GPA620V	Bedford YMT	Duple Dominant	C53F	1980	Ex Porter, Dunmer, 1986
12	TBD618N	Bedford YRT	Willowbrook	B53F	1974	Ex Athelstan, Malmesbury, 1987
14	GGR344N	Bedford YRQ	Willowbrook	B47F	1974	Ex Gastonia, Cranleigh, 1987
18	E318SYG	Mercedes-Benz 811D	Optare StarRider	B33F	1988	
19	MPE248P	Bedford YRQ	Plaxton Derwent	B49F	1976	Ex Farnham Coaches, 1988
20	VDL264K	Bedford YRQ	Plaxton Derwent	B49F	1972	Ex Gale, Haslemere, 1988
24	F70RPL	Mercedes-Benz 811D	Optare StarRider	DP33F	1989	
25	G301CPL	Mercedes-Benz 811D	Optare StarRider	B33F	1989	
26	G972WPA	Optare MetroRider	Optare	B33F	1990	
27	UGB14R	AEC Reliance 6U3ZR	Duple Dominant	C53F	1977	Ex Moss, Sandown, 1990
29	H743LHN	CVE Omni	Omni	B23F	1990	
30	H744LHN	CVE Omni	Omni	B21FL	1990	
31	H745LHN	CVE Omni	Omni	B21FL	1990	
32	OHV208Y	Ford R1114	Wadham Stringer	B32F	1982	
33	YLN636S	Ford R1014	Duple Dominant	B47F	1978	Ex LB of Hillingdon, 1991
34	J326PPD	Optare MetroRider	Optare	B33F	1991	
35	VNU533Y	Ford R1014	Duple Dominant	B47F	1982	Ex Lamcote, Redcliffe, 1991
36	J752PPM	Dennis Dart 9.8SDL	Wadham Stringer	B37F	1991	Ex Wadham Stringer, 1991
37	D602RGJ	Bedford YMT	Plaxton Derwent	B53F	1987	Ex Epsom Buses, 1991
38	D167TAU	Bedford YMT	Duple Dominant	B55F	1986	Ex National Plant, 1992
39	KFH933P	Bedford YRQ	Plaxton Supreme	C45F	1975	
40	B88BVW	Ford R1015	Wadham Stringer Vanguard	B33F	1984	Ex Wealden, Nettlestead, 1992
41	C913BYP	Bedford YMT	Wadham Stringer Vanguard	B41F	1986	Ex Wealden, Nettlestead, 1992

EASTONWAYS Fleet List

EUI1586	Leyland Leopard PSU3B/4R	Plaxton Elite III	C51F	1973	Ex Kemp, Chillenden, 1989
GBZ7129	Leyland Leopard PSU3B/4R	Duple Dominant	C51F	1974	Ex Fylde, 1991
EUI1587	Ford R1114	Duple Dominant	C53F	1976	Ex Horseshoe, Kemston, 1990
GBZ7128	Leyland Leopard PSU3E/4R	Duple Dominant II	C53F	1978	Ex Kemp, Chillenden, 1991
SAD121R	Leyland Leopard PSU3E/4R	Duple Dominant II	C53F	1978	Ex Wealdon Beeline, 1992
A994THJ	Leyland Cub CU435	Wadham Stringer Vanguard	B33FL	1984	Ex London Borough of Redbridge, 1992
C449SJU	Ford Transit VE6	Robin Hood	B16F	1985	Ex Lea, Emsworth, 1991
F726EKR	Ford Transit VE6	Dormobile	C16F	1988	
J998LKR	OBC Omni	OBC	DP21F	1991	

Previous Registrations:

EUI1586	KBU895L	GBZ7128	VYK201S
EUI1587	PKX262R	GBZ7129	YNA398M

Named Vehicles:
EUI1586 *Duchess of Kent*, EUI1587 *Duke of Kent*, GBX7128 *Princess of Kent*, GBX7129 *Prince of Kent*, SAD121R *Maid of Kent*.

FARLEIGH COACHES Fleet List

VJG187J	AEC Swift 5P2R	Marshall	B51F	1970	Ex Blue Birds Majorettes, Maidstone, 1987
JGF410K	Daimler Fleetline CRG6LXB	Park Royal	H44/29F	1972	Ex Tellyn, Little Baddow, 1983
WFS288K	Leyland Atlantean PDR1A/1	Alexander J	H45/33F	1972	Ex Ulsterbus, 1990
PNU115K	Leyland Atlantean PDR1A/1	Roe	H42/29D	1972	Ex Rose, Walderslade, 1990
KRL420P	Bedford YRQ	Duple Dominant	B47F	1975	Ex Western National, 1989
THX140S	Leyland National 10351A/2R		B36D	1977	Ex London Buses, 1991
JIA2801	Ford Transit 190	Dormobile	B16F	1979	Ex Sowery, Headcorn, 1991
BTH364V	AEC Reliance 6U3ZR	Duple Dominant II Express	C53F	1979	Ex Steel, Addingham, 1991
NMJ291V	AEC Reliance 6U3ZR	Van Hool Aragon	C53F	1979	Ex Horlock, Northfleet, 1991
C348RPE	Ford Transit 190	Carlyle	B16F	1986	Ex Alder Valley, 1988
F438RRY	DAF SB2305DHS585	Caetano Algarve	C53F	1989	

Previous Registrations:

JIA2801	FKX150T

127

FUGGLES Fleet List

Reg	Chassis	Body	Seats	Year	History
AKM425K	Leyland Leopard PSU4A/2R	Willowbrook	B52F	1971	Ex Wealden PSV, Nettlestead, 1990
STD119L	Leyland Leopard PSU4B/2R	Seddon Pennine	B47F	1972	Ex Maidstone, 1982
LUG523P	Leyland Leopard PSU4C/4R	Plaxton Derwent	B52F	1976	Ex Wealden, Five Oak Green, 1992
RAW29R	Bedford YLQ	Duple Dominant II	C45F	1977	Ex Morgan, Ingatestone, 1990
SKN910R	Leyland National 11351A/1R		DP48F	1977	Ex Hastings & District, 1989
SKN911R	Leyland National 11351A/1R		DP46F	1977	Ex Hastings & District, 1989
UFT911T	Bedford YLQ	Plaxton Supreme III	C45F	1978	Ex Rowland & Goodwin, 1983
HVC10V	Bedford YMT	Plaxton Supreme IV	C53F	1979	Ex Rowland & Goodwin, 1984
GKK160V	Leyland Leopard PSU3E/4R	Willowbrook 003 MKII	C49F	1980	Ex New Enterprise, Chatham, 1991
NKY275X	Mercedes-Benz L207D	Whittaker-Europa	B12F	1982	Ex Goulding, Knottingley, 1987
BUT47Y	Bedford YNT	Plaxton Paramount 3200 Ex	C53F	1983	Ex Wainfleet, Nuneaton, 1987
B420CMC	Mercedes-Benz L608D	Reeve Burgess	C21F	1985	Ex Garcia, London W2, 1989
F981HGE	Volvo B10M-60	Plaxton Paramount 3500 III	C49FT	1989	Ex Park, Hamilton, 1990
J996MKM	OBC Omni	OBC	DP20F	1991	Ex Wealden Beeline, 1992

HANTS & SUSSEX / SOUTHERN MOTORWAYS Fleet List

Reg	Chassis	Body	Seats	Year	History
VLW217G	AEC Merlin 4P2R	MCW	B41D	1968	Ex Mobil Oil, Coryton, 1989
VLW529G	AEC Merlin 4P2R	MCW	B50F	1969	Ex Clifton College, Bristol, 1989
AML97H	AEC Swift 4MP2R	Park Royal	B32D	1969	Ex P&O, Dover, 1989
AML567H	AEC Merlin 4P2R	MCW	B50F	1969	Ex P&O, Dover, 1989
AML570H	AEC Merlin 4P2R	MCW	B47D	1969	Ex Harris, Dunkirk, 1990
AML601H	AEC Merlin 4P2R	MCW	B50F	1969	Ex Buckland & Hetherington, 1992
BPH111H	AEC Swift 4MP2R	Park Royal	B47F	1970	Ex Venture, Harrow, 1988
BPH114H	AEC Swift 4MP2R	Park Royal	B43F	1970	Ex London Country, 1985
BPH144H	AEC Swift 4MP2R	Park Royal	B43F	1970	Ex London Country, 1987
DPD502J	AEC Swift 4MP2R	MCW	B43D	1971	Ex Gatwick Handling, Gatwick, 1986
EGN683J	AEC Swift 4MP2R	MCW	B43F	1971	Ex preservation, 1988
LRV978	Leyland Leopard PSU3B/4R	Plaxton Elite Express III	C51F	1973	Ex Southampton, 1990
KKW66P	Leyland Leopard PSU3C/4R	Alexander AY	DP49F	1976	Ex West Riding, 1990
NUR82P	Leyland Leopard PSU5A/4R	Plaxton Supreme III	C50F	1978	Ex Hallums, Southend, 1991
135MHT	Leyland Leopard PSU3E/4R	Plaxton Supreme IV	C53F	1978	Ex Shamrock & Rambler, 1988
WRO434S	Leyland Leopard PSU3E/4R	Duple Dominant II	C53F	1978	Ex Southend, 1988
CTM406T	Leyland Leopard PSU3E/4R	Duple Dominant II	C53F	1979	Ex Southend, 1988
CTM407T	Leyland Leopard PSU3E/4R	Duple Dominant II	C53F	1979	Ex Southend, 1988
GGS927T	Ford R1114	Duple Dominant II	C53F	1979	
JMJ108V	Ford R1114	Duple Dominant II	C53F	1979	
JMJ109V	Ford R1114	Duple Dominant II	C53F	1979	

Previous Registrations:

135MHT	WOC729T	LRV978	FEL104L

HAVEN COACHES Fleet List

Reg	Chassis	Body	Seats	Year	History
WLT933	AEC Routemaster 5RM	Park Royal	H36/28R	1961	Ex Western Scottish, 1991
WLT960	AEC Routemaster 5RM	Park Royal	H36/28R	1961	Ex Western Scottish, 1991
YWE514M	Leyland Leopard PSU3B/4R	Plaxton Elite III	C53F	1973	Ex Allen, Sittingbourne, 1992
GHV20N	Daimler Fleetline CRL6	Park Royal	H45/28D	1974	Ex Frontrunner, Dagenham, 1991
RCN97N	Leyland Atlantean AN68/1R	Park Royal	H43/34F	1974	Ex Allen, Sole Street, 1991
KUC133P	Daimler Fleetline CRL6	Park Royal	H45/28D	1975	Ex Frontrunner, Dagenham, 1991
THX180S	Leyland National 10351A/2R		B36D	1978	Ex Allen, Sittingbourne, 1992
THX230S	Leyland National 10351A/2R		B36D	1978	Ex Telling-Golden Miller, 1992
E106SOG	Freight Rover Sherpa 374	Carlyle	B20F	1987	Ex Allen, Sittingbourne, 1992

INLAND TRAVEL Fleet List

VKE569S	Leyland National 11351A/1R		B49F	1977	Ex East Midland, 1992
HR55	Bedford YMT	Plaxton Supreme IV	C53F	1979	Ex Windsorian, Windsor, 1991
DKG270V	Bedford YMT	Plaxton Supreme IV	C53F	1980	Ex Windsorian, Windsor, 1991
ROF882	Auwaerter Neoplan N122/3	Auwaerter Skyliner	CH57/20CT	1984	

Previous Registrations:

HR55	YJB331T	ROF882	B173BFE

KENT COACH TOURS Fleet List

UUR349W	Leyland Leopard PSU5C/4R	Plaxton Supreme IV	C57F	1981	Ex Chambers, Stevenage, 1991
EBD181X	Leyland Leopard PSU3G/4RT	Eastern Coach Works	C49F	1982	Ex Hill, Congleton, 1990
LAG313Y	Leyland Tiger TRCTL11/3R	Plaxton Paramount 3500	C50F	1983	Ex Dorset Travel, 1991
KCT638	Leyland Tiger TRCTL11/3R	Plaxton Paramount 3500	C48FT	1983	Ex Dorset Travel, 1991
A41SKL	Ford R1115	Plaxton Paramount 3200 E	C53F	1984	Ex Andrews, Trudoxhill, 1989
KCT986	Bova FHD12-280	Bova Futura	C48FT	1985	Ex Truelove, Liversedge, 1988
D772PTU	Freight Rover Sherpa 365	Dormobile	B16F	1986	Ex Crosville, 1990

Previous Registrations:

A41SKL	A56HAD, KCT638	KCT986	B556KRY
KCT638	EWW951Y	LAG313Y	GRH2Y

MARCHWOOD MOTORWAYS Fleet List

213	H711LOL	Dennis Dart 9SDL3002	Carlyle Dartline	B36F	1990	
214	H712LOL	Dennis Dart 9.8SDL3004	Carlyle Dartline	B40F	1991	
288	D647ETR	Iveco Daily 49.10	Robin Hood	B17F	1987	
289	D648ETR	Iveco Daily 49.10	Robin Hood	B19F	1987	
290	F730OOT	Iveco Daily 49.10	Robin Hood	B23F	1988	
291	F731OOT	Iveco Daily 49.10	Robin Hood	B23F	1988	

408-416

	Leyland National 11351A/1R		B49F	1976	Ex Solent Blue Line, 1988

408	PJT262R	409	PJT264R	413	PJT271R	414	RJT149R	416	UFX850S

502	F246RJX	DAF SB220LC550	Optare Delta	B47F	1989
503	J45GCX	DAF SB220LC550	Optare Delta	B49F	1992

UNP996L	Bedford YRT	Duple Dominant	C53F	1973	Ex Pangbourne Coaches, 1985
JTY925P	Bedford YRT	Plaxton Elite	C53F	1975	Ex Pangbourne Coaches, 1985
VTA989S	Bedford YMT	Plaxton Supreme	C53F	1977	Ex Yendell, Witheridge, 1986
CEL105T	Bedford YMT	Plaxton Supreme	C53F	1979	Ex Day, North Common, 1986
VFB615T	Bedford YMT	Caetano Algarve	C53F	1979	Ex Frayer, Bristol, 1986
BHO440V	Leyland Leopard PSU5C/4R	Duple Dominant II	C55F	1980	
225ASV	Bova EL26/581	Bova Europa	C52F	1982	Ex Dodsworth, Scarborough, 1989
228ASV	Bova EL26/581	Bova Europa	C52F	1982	Ex Dodsworth, Scarborough, 1989
UFX630X	Leyland Tiger TRCTL11/3R	Duple Caribbean	C57F	1981	
CFX424Y	DAF SB2300DHS585	LAG	C53F	1983	
CFX425Y	DAF SB2300DHS585	LAG	C53F	1983	
CLJ920Y	DAF SB2300DHS585	LAG	C53F	1983	
C82NNV	DAF SB2300DKSB	Caetano Algarve	C49F	1985	
C83NNV	DAF SB2300DKSB	Caetano Algarve	C53F	1986	
C337VRY	Bova FHD12/250	Bova Futura	C57F	1986	
D131CJF	Bova FHD12/290	Bova Futura	C53F	1987	
D258JPR	Ford Transit 190	Deansgate	B12F	1987	
D259JPR	Ford Transit 190	Deansgate	B12F	1987	
E523TOV	Iveco Daily 49.10	Carlyle Dailybus II	B25F	1988	Ex Hornsby, Ashby, 1991
F247RJX	DAF SB2305DHT585	Duple 340	C57F	1989	
F248RJX	DAF SB2305DHT585	Duple 340	C57F	1989	
F629SRP	LAG Panoramic	LAG	C53F	1989	
F630SRP	LAG Panoramic	LAG	C53F	1989	
F764XNH	LAG Panoramic	LAG	C53F	1989	

F851YJX	DAF SB2305DHTD585	Plaxton Paramount 3500	C53F	1989	
F432YFX	Ford Transit VE6	Ford	B11F	1989	
G468BTR	Ford Transit VE6	Ford	B11F	1990	
G364FOP	Iveco Daily 49.10	Carlyle Dailybus II	B25F	1989	Ex Strathclyde's Buses, 1991
G211VPX	DAF Sherpa 400	DAF	B16F	1989	
G722VTR	DAF Sherpa 400	DAF	B16F	1989	
G502WOR	DAF Sherpa 200	DAF	B12F	1990	
H391CJF	MAN 10-180	Caetano ??	C35F	1990	
H186EJF	Toyota HB31R	Caetano Optimo	C21F	1991	
H187EJF	Toyota HB31R	Caetano Optimo	C18F	1991	
H975EOR	Iveco Daily 49.10	Pheonix	B25F	1991	
H51VNH	Volvo B10M-60	Jonckheere Jubilee P50	C51FT	1990	
H52VNH	Volvo B10M-60	Jonckheere Jubilee P50	C51FT	1990	
J851KHD	DAF SB2305DHS585	Van Hool Alizée	C49FT	1992	
J852KHD	DAF SB2305DHS585	Van Hool Alizée	C49FT	1992	
J853KHD	DAF SB2305DHS585	Van Hool Alizée	C49FT	1992	
J854KHD	DAF SB2305DHS585	Plaxton Paramount 3500	C55F	1992	

Previous Registrations:

225ASV	SMY621X		228ASV	SMY628X

Special Liveries:

Totton-Link:	D647/8ETR

MERCURY PASSENGER SERVICES Fleet List

JJG5P	Leyland Atlantean AN68/1R	Eastern Coach Works	H43/31F	1976	Ex Eastbourne, 1992
JJG888P	Leyland National 11351/1R		B49F	1976	Ex East Kent, 1991
OUC105R	Scania BR111DH	MCW Metropolitan	H43/29D	1976	Ex Reading, 1992
PJJ342S	Leyland National 10351A/1R		B41F	1977	Ex East Kent, 1991
D338JUM	Volkswagen LT55	Optare City Pacer	B25F	1986	Ex London Buses, 1991
D361JUM	Volkswagen LT55	Optare City Pacer	B25F	1986	Ex London Buses, 1991
D813KWT	Freight Rover Sherpa 374	Dormobile	B16F	1987	Ex West Riding, 1991

NU-VENTURE Fleet List

PTT106R	Bristol LH6L	Plaxton Supreme III Exp	C43F	1977	Ex Worthington, Collingham, 1989
3558RU	Leyland Tiger TRCTL11/3R	Duple Laser	C51F	1983	Ex Warren, Neath, 1991
8421RU	Leyland Royal Tiger B50	Plaxton Paramount 3500	C49FT	1984	Ex Lumb, Birstall, 1990
A157MNE	Leyland Tiger TRCTL11/3RZ	Duple Laser	C53F	1984	Ex Shearings, 1991
E134NDE	Peugeot-Talbot Pullman	Talbot	B22F	1988	Ex Tenby Bus & Coach, 1990
G92SKR	Dennis Javelin 12SDA1907	Caetano Algarve	C51FT	1990	
G75TKN	Peugeot-Talbot Pullman	Talbot	DP22F	1990	
H192EKM	Peugeot-Talbot Pullman	Talbot	B22F	1991	

Previous Registrations:

3558RU	HBH427Y, 9GUV, SWN753Y		8421RU	A323XHE

PRIORY COACHES Fleet List

BXM568	Bedford WTL	Duple	C20F	1935	Ex Mitchham Belle, 19??
MLK702L	Ford Transit 190	Strachans	B16F	1972	Ex London Transport, 1980
OTO577M	Leyland Atlantean AN68/1R	East Lancashire	H44/33D	1973	Ex Nottingham, 1988
RNV809M	Bristol VRT/SL6G	Eastern Coach Works	H41/31F	1973	Ex Talbot, Cowplain, 1990
TPD185M	Leyland National 1051/1R/0402		B41F	1973	Ex London Country NW, 1990
UPE202M	Leyland National 1051/1R		B41F	1973	Ex London Country NW, 1988
HWC38N	Leyland National 11351/1R		B49F	1974	Ex Solent Blue Line, 1991
JTH756P	Leyland National 11351/1R		B52F	1974	Ex Solent Blue Line, 1991
LBH944P	Ford R1114	Duple Dominant	C53F	1976	Ex K-line, London E10, 1989
DHE673V	Ford R1114	Plaxton Supreme	C53F	1979	Ex Horseman, Reading, 1992
EDP901V	Ford Transit 190	Dormobile	B16F	1979	Ex Horseman, Reading, 1992
JBH388V	Ford R1014	Duple Dominant	C35F	1979	Ex Horseman, Reading, 1992
KNT815W	Bedford CFL	Plaxton	C17F	1980	Ex Holmes, Lee-on-Solent, 1992

GOT61X	Mercedes-Benz L508D	Robin Hood	C19F	1981	Ex Easson, Southampton, 1991
MRX271X	Mercedes-Benz L508D	Devon Conversions	C19F	1981	Ex Horseman, Reading, 1992
OAN253X	Mercedes-Benz L508D	Devon Conversions	C19F	1982	Ex Horseman, Reading, 1992
PPH277X	Leyland Leopard PSU5C/4R	Duple Dominant	C57F	1982	
URW701X	Ford R1014	Plaxton Supreme	C35F	1981	Ex Bonas, Coventry, 1983
A675DCN	Leyland Tiger TRCTL11/3R	Plaxton Paramount 3500	C50F	1984	Ex Northumbria, 1991
A695DCN	Leyland Tiger TRCTL11/3R	Plaxton Paramount 3500	C50F	1984	Ex Northumbria, 1991
A696DCN	Leyland Tiger TRCTL11/3R	Plaxton Paramount 3500	C50F	1984	Ex Northumbria, 1991
A36GJT	Leyland Tiger TRCTL11/3R	Plaxton Paramount 3200	C57F	1983	Ex Brockhurst, Maudlin, 1987
B826KRY	Leyland Tiger TRCTL11/3R	Plaxton Paramount 3200	C53F	1984	Ex Negrotti, Greenford, 1989
B263VOR	Bova EL26/581	Bova Europa 3	C53F	1984	
C33VJF	Bova FHD12/280	Bova Futura	C49FT	1986	Ex Garratt, Newton Abbot, 1992
C550WAC	Bova FHD12/280	Bova Futura	C53F	1986	Ex Lewis, Greenwich, 1991
D620WPJ	Kässbohrer Setra S215HD	Kässbohrer Tornado	C49FT	1986	Ex Kässbohrer UK, 1987
TSU608	Kässbohrer Setra S210HD	Kässbohrer Tornado	C35F	1987	Ex Gale, Haslemere, 1990
D881MWR	Freight Rover Sherpa 374	Dormobile	B20F	1987	Ex Yorkshire Rider, 1990
E986NMK	Mercedes-Benz 609D	Reeve Burgess	DP25F	1988	
E184KHD	Bova FHD12/290	Bova Futura	C49FT	1988	Ex Lyles, Batley, 1991
G95VFP	Bova FHD12/280	Bova Futura	C57F	1989	
G96VFP	Bova FHD12/280	Bova Futura	C57F	1989	
G423WFP	Bova FHD12/280	Bova Futura	C53F	1989	Ex Moseley demonstrator, 1990
H326DTR	Volvo B10M-60	Plaxton Expressliner	C49FT	1991	
J260MFP	Leyland Tiger TRCL10/3AZRM	Plaxton Paramount 3500 III	C57F	1991	
J461JRV	Bova FHD12/290	Bova Futura	C57F	1992	

Previous Registrations:

A696DCN	A32FVN, GSU348	A695DCN	A31FVN, GSU347
A675DCN	A30FVN, GSU346	TSU608	D907APM

Special Liveries:

ABC Coaches:	LBH944P, TSU608
Overall Advert:	RNV809M
National Express:	A695/6DCN, H326DTR

POYNTER'S Fleet List

NFM831M	Leyland National 1151/1R/0405		DP48F	1973	Ex Seabrook, Hythe, 1991
YBM938S	DAF MB200DKL600	Plaxton Supreme	C57F	1978	Ex Wells, Brixham, 1990
HMA562T	Leyland National 10351B/1R		B44F	1978	Ex Crosville Wales, 1991
GMB665T	Leyland National 10351B/1R		B44F	1978	Ex Crosville Wales, 1991
FTO562V	Bedford YMT	Plaxton Supreme IV Express	C53F	1979	Ex Allen, Sittingbourne, 1989
CVA404V	Bedford YMT	Plaxton Supreme IV Express	C53F	1980	Ex Burton, Haverhill, 1989
LLL173V	Ford Transit 190	Robin Hood	C16F	1980	Ex Capital, West Drayton, 1986
3318VU	MAN SR280	MAN	C53F	1981	Ex Clark & Ellwood, Chatteris, 1991
YKY777	Bova EL26/581	Bova Europa	C53F	1982	Ex UMBH, Southend, 1990
8465LJ	DAF SB2300DHS585	Berkhof Esprite 350	C49FT	1983	Ex Travelfar, Henfield, 1991
6769FM	DAF SB2305DHS585	Berkhof Esprite 340	C49FT	1984	Ex UMBH, Southend, 1990
2448UE	DAF SB2300DHS585	Berkhof Esprite 340	C49FT	1985	Ex Travelfar, Henfield, 1991
C424AHT	Ford Transit 190	Carlyle	B16F	1986	Ex Pickford, Grittleton, 1991
D856OJA	Mercedes-Benz 609D	Made-to-Measure	C27F	1987	Ex Mitchell, Plean, 1989

Previous Registrations:

2448UE	B688BTW	6769FM	A166OHJ	YKY777	DHK456X
3318VU	CCA773X	8465LJ	LHK645Y		

RAMBLER Fleet List

01	LYC731	Bedford OB	Duple Bella Vista	C29F	1950	Ex preservation, 1983
02	EDY565E	Bedford VAM14	Duple Bella Vista	C45F	1967	Ex Plumridge, Horley, 1980
03	ECB791W	Bedford YMQ	Duple Dominant II	C45F	1980	Ex Turner, Chulmleigh, 1984
04	WUF44	Bedford YMT	Duple Dominant	C53F	1976	
06	PKO260W	Bedford YMT	Duple Dominant II	C53F	1980	Ex Moore & Verge, Cliftenville, 1992
07	710VCV	Bedford YMT	Duple Dominant II	C53F	1980	Ex WMH, Hutton, 1990
10	CKN142Y	Bedford YMT	Wright TT	DP53F	1982	Ex Boro'line, 1992
11	CKN143Y	Bedford YMT	Wright TT	DP53F	1982	Ex Boro'line, 1992
12	MGS437V	Bedford YLQ	Alexander AY(1973)	DP45F	1976	Ex O'Neill, Gillingham, 1991
14	WNH52W	Bedford YMQS	Lex Maxeta	B33F	1981	Ex Milton Keynes City Bus, 1987

15	TCD481J	Bristol RESL6L	Marshall Camagna Two	B45F	1970	Ex Farmer, Ashford, 1990
16	D941UDY	Freight Rover Sherpa 374	Made-to-Measure	C16F	1986	
17	BYJ967Y	Volvo B10M-61	Plaxton Paramount 3500	C53F	1983	Ex Coliseum, West End, 1989
18	LDY173	Volvo B10M-61	Van Hool Alizée	C53FT	1988	
19	SDY788	Volvo B10M-61	Van Hool Alizée	C53F	1987	Ex Shearings, 1992
20	910OCV	Bedford YNT	Duple Dominant II	C53F	1977	Ex Coliseum, West End, 1990
21	TAP461R	Bedford YMT	Plaxton Supreme Express	C53F	1976	Ex Morgan, Nantyglo, 1987
22	NCF715	Bedford YMT	Plaxton Supreme IV	C53F	1979	Ex Young, Rampton, 1989
23	405UPJ	Bedford YMT	Plaxton Supreme IV	C53F	1980	Ex Watson, Annfield Plain, 1987
24	EYL319V	Bedford YMT	Plaxton Supreme	C53F	1978	Ex ROF Bishopton, 1991
27	UDY512	Volvo B10M-60	Plaxton Paramount 3500 III	C51FT	1989	Ex Park, Hamilton, 1991
28	NDY820	Volvo B10M-60	Plaxton Paramount 3500 III	C51FT	1989	Ex Park, Hamilton, 1991
31	1924RH	Bedford YNT	Plaxton Paramount 3200	C50F	1983	Ex Taylor, Meppershall, 1991
32	GDY473	Dennis Javelin 12SDA1907	Plaxton Paramount 3200 III	C53F	1989	Ex Elizabethan Travel, 1991
33	UDY910	Bedford YMPS	Plaxton Paramount 3200 III	C33F	1987	
34	RDY155	Bedford YMPS	Plaxton Paramount 3200 III	C33F	1987	
35	TDY388	Volvo B10M-60	Plaxton Paramount 3500 III	C51FT	1990	
37	HDY405	Volvo B10M-61	Plaxton Paramount 3500 III	C51FT	1987	
38	FDY83	Volvo B10M-61	Plaxton Paramount 3500 II	C51FT	1986	

Previous Registrations:

1924RH	JNM744Y, 617MUA, KUR585Y	LDY173	E184XJK
405UPJ	JJF880V, SDY788	NCF715	YEB105T
710VCV	DMT904V	NDY820	F28HGG
910VCV	OTR412S	RDY155	D134VJK
A673NJK	A888MDY, NDY820	TAP461R	OTX41R, 419CLB
BYJ967Y	LTR444Y, 800GTA, 910VCV	SDY788	D588MVR
EUF738L	RTB222L, 1924RH	TDY388	G135UWV
FDY83	C588SJK	UDY512	F27HGG
GDY473	G168ODH	UDY910	D133VJK
HDY405	D137VJK	WUF44	LJK335P

RYE COACHES Fleet List

NWO491R	Leyland National 11351A/1R		B52F	1976	Ex National Welsh, 1990
PDK309S	Bedford YMT	Duple Dominant II	C53F	1977	Ex Campbell & White-Hide, Bexhill, 1990
AYJ987T	Bedford YMT	Duple Dominant II	C53F	1979	Ex Campbell & White-Hide, Bexhill, 1990
CWG746V	Leyland Atlantean AN68A/1R	Roe	H45/29D	1979	Ex South Yorkshire, 1991
CWG757V	Leyland Atlantean AN68A/1R	Roe	H45/29D	1979	Ex South Yorkshire, 1991
LKN585W	Ford Transit 190	Williams Deansgate	B12C	1980	Ex Young, Bearsted, 1990
WRP226W	Volvo B10M-61	Duple Dominant IV	C48FT	1981	Ex York, Cogenhoe, 1990

SAFEGUARD Fleet List

GPG342V	Leyland Leopard PSU3E/4R	Duple Dominant	B53F	1980	
NPD689W	Leyland Leopard PSU3F/4R	Duple Dominant	B53F	1981	
TPA968X	Leyland Leopard PSU3E/4R	Duple Dominant	B53F	1981	
YPD217Y	Leyland Leopard PSU3G/4R	Duple Dominant	B53F	1982	
KUS244Y	Leyland Tiger TRBTL11/2R	Duple Dominant	B53F	1982	Ex Hutchison, Overtown, 1986
247FCG	Kässbohrer Setra S215HD	Kässbohrer Tornado	C49FT	1982	Ex Farnham Coaches, 1988
515FCG	Kässbohrer Setra S215HR	Kässbohrer Rational	C53F	1982	Ex Farnham Coaches, 1988
531FCG	Kässbohrer Setra S215HD	Kässbohrer Tornado	C49FT	1983	Ex Farnham Coaches, 1988
A60GPL	Mercedes-Benz L608D	Reeve Burgess	C19F	1984	
A62HPG	Leyland Tiger TRCTL11/3R	Plaxton Paramount 3200	C53F	1984	
B906SPR	Volvo B10M-61	Plaxton Paramount 3200	C53F	1984	Ex Excelsior, Bournemouth, 1986
B907SPR	Volvo B10M-61	Plaxton Paramount 3200	C53F	1984	Ex Excelsior, Bournemouth, 1986
277FCG	Kässbohrer Setra S215HR	Kässbohrer Rational	C53F	1984	Ex Farnham Coaches, 1988
C164SPB	Leyland Tiger TRBTL11/2R	Duple Dominant	B53F	1985	
DSK559	Kässbohrer Setra S215HR	Kässbohrer Rational	C49FT	1986	Ex Tourswift, Birtley, 1990
DSK560	Leyland Tiger TRBTL11/2RZ	Plaxton Paramount 3500	C48F	1986	
C105AFX	Volvo B10M-61	Plaxton Paramount 3200	C53F	1986	Ex Excelsior, Bournemouth, 1986
D123HML	Mercedes-Benz L608D	Reeve Burgess	C19F	1986	
D159HML	Mercedes-Benz 609D	Reeve Burgess	B20F	1986	
D633XVV	Volkswagen LT55	Optare City Pacer	B25F	1986	Ex Leicester, 1991
538FCG	Leyland Tiger TRCTL11/3R	Duple 320	C57F	1987	Ex Pan Atlas, London W3, 1988
D165HML	Leyland Lynx LX112TL11FR1	Leyland	B49F	1987	

E51MMT	Leyland Lynx LX112TL11FR1S	Leyland	B49F	1987	
159FCG	Kässbohrer Setra S215HD	Kässbohrer Tornado	C47FT	1987	Ex Farnham Coaches, 1988
E297OMG	Leyland Lynx LX112L10ZR1R	Leyland	B49F	1988	
E298OMG	Leyland Lynx LX112L10ZR1R	Leyland	B49F	1988	
F296RMH	Volvo B10M-46	Plaxton Paramount 3200 III	C39F	1988	
DSK558	TAZ	TAZ Dubrava D3200	C49FT	1989	Ex Thandi, Bearwood, 1990
F474WFX	Volvo B10M-60	Plaxton Paramount 3200 III	C57F	1989	Ex Excelsior, Bournemouth, 1989
F475WFX	Volvo B10M-60	Plaxton Paramount 3200 III	C53F	1989	Ex Excelsior, Bournemouth, 1989
G514EFX	Volvo B10M-60	Plaxton Paramount 3200 III	C53F	1990	Ex Excelsior, Bournemouth, 1991
G520EFX	Volvo B10M-60	Plaxton Paramount 3200 III	C53F	1990	Ex Excelsior, Bournemouth, 1990

Previous Registrations:

247FCG	RAX22Y	538FCG	D145HML	DSK559	C665UPJ
515FCG	UPB669X	DSK558	F794TBC	DSK560	C270TPL
531FCG	APA672Y				

SMITH'S Fleet List

JG9938	Leyland Tiger TS8	Park Royal	C32R	1937	Ex preservation, 1988
KJD552P	Leyland National 10351A/2R		B36D	1976	Ex London Buses, 1989
SKJ597R	Ford R1114	Duple Dominant I	C53F	1977	
ODL885R	Leyland National 10351A/1R		B44F	1977	Ex Southern Vectis, 1987
ODL888R	Leyland National 10351A/1R		B44F	1977	Ex Southern Vectis, 1987
PTD669S	Leyland National 11351A/1R		B49F	1978	Ex Greater Manchester, 1987
THX143S	Leyland National 10351A/2R		B36D	1978	Ex London Buses, 1990
AKL639T	Ford R1114	Duple Dominant II Exp	C53F	1978	
AKL640T	Ford R1114	Duple Dominant II Exp	C53F	1978	
GKM615V	Ford R1114	Plaxton Supreme IV Exp	C53F	1979	
GKM616V	Ford R1114	Plaxton Supreme IV Exp	C53F	1979	
JFD288V	Ford R1114	Duple Dominant II	C53F	1979	Ex Olsen, Strood, 1980
JFD293V	Ford R1114	Duple Dominant II	C53F	1979	Ex Olsen, Strood, 1982
OHA467W	Ford R1114	Plaxton Supreme IV	C53F	1980	Ex Parry, Cheslyn Hay, 1982
YBA552Y	Ford Transit 190	Ford-Crystals	B12F	1981	
A638LKO	Ward Dalesman TV8-640	Plaxton Paramount 3200	C57F	1983	
NIB3834	MCW Metroliner DR130/3	MCW	CH57/23F	1984	Ex Ambassador Travel, 1990
B164TKL	Leyland Tiger TRCTL11/3R	Plaxton Paramount 3200	C57F	1984	
LIB7133	Leyland Tiger TRCTL11/3R	Plaxton Paramount 3500	C53F	1984	Ex Hills, Tredegar, 1988
LIB7134	Leyland Tiger TRCTL11/3R	Plaxton Paramount 3500	C53F	1984	Ex Hills, Tredegar, 1988
B46XKJ	Leyland Tiger TRCTL11/3R	Plaxton Paramount 3500	C53F	1985	
MIB526	Leyland Royal Tiger RTC	Leyland Doyen	C48FT	1986	Ex Fishwick, Leyland, 1988
E720VKE	Talbot Express	Crystals	C14F	1987	
E75VKO	Leyland Tiger TRCTL11/3RZ	Plaxton Paramount 3200 III	C57F	1987	
E76VKO	Leyland Tiger TRCTL11/3RZ	Plaxton Paramount 3200 III	C57F	1987	
F22YBO	Kässbohrer Setra S215HDI	Kässbohrer Tornado	C49FT	1989	Ex Bebb, Llantwit Fardre, 1991

Previous Registrations:

LIB7133	A782WHB		MIB526	C752MFR
LIB7134	A586WNY		NIB3834	A119KBA

Named Vehicles: F22YBO *Pride of Swale*

SUSSEX BUS Fleet List

TCD490J	Bristol RESL6L	Marshall	B45F	1970	Ex Wealden, Five Oak Green, 1991
SJA352K	Bristol RELL6L	Marshall	B49F	1971	Ex Citybus, Middleton, 1989
XSU682	Leyland Leopard PSU3B/4R	Willowbrook Warrior (1990)	B49F	1973	Ex Danks, Oldfield, 1991
SSU780W	Leyland Leopard PSU3E/4R	Duple Dominant	B55F	1973	Ex Graham, Paisley, 1990
JTM109V	AEC Reliance 6U3ZR	Duple Dominant	B53F	1979	Ex Tillingbourne, 1992
HSC171X	Leyland Cub CU435	Duple Dominant	B31F	1981	Ex Lothian, 1991
CSU992	Leyland Leopard PSU3E/4R	Willowbrook Warrior (1990)	B47F	1979	Ex SUT, 1990
XSU612	Leyland Leopard PSU3F/4R	Willowbrook Warrior (1990)	B48F	1981	Ex Battrick, Blackburn, 1990

Previous Registrations:

CSU992	OMA506V, TCS157	XSU612	PWT238W	XSU682	OKG158M

THANET BUS Fleet List

Reg	Chassis	Body	Seating	Year	History
RUF41R	Leyland National 11351A/2R		DP52F	1977	Ex McColl, Bowling, 1992
NEN954R	Leyland National 11351A/1R		B49F	1977	Ex Green, Kirkintilloch, 1991
NEN958R	Leyland National 11351A/1R		B49F	1977	Ex Green, Kirkintilloch, 1991
NEN963R	Leyland National 11351A/1R		B49F	1977	Ex Green, Kirkintilloch, 1991
VPT946R	Leyland National 11351A/1R		B49F	1977	Ex McColl, Bowling, 1992
PTD671S	Leyland National 11351A/1R		DP49F	1978	Ex Green, Kirkintilloch, 1991
XNG773S	Leyland National 11351A/1R		B49F	1978	Ex Green, Kirkintilloch, 1991
BPT902S	Leyland National 11351A/1R		B49F	1978	Ex Marbill, Beith, 1991
YKN825S	Bedford YMT	Duple Dominant	B61F	1978	Ex Boro'line Maidstone, 1991
PVY767T	Bedford YMT	Duple Dominant	B63F	1979	Ex Redby, Sunderland, 1991
WBN478T	Leyland National 11351A/1R		B49F	1979	Ex Green, Kirkintilloch, 1991
REP328Y	Leyland Tiger TRCTL11/2R	Plaxton Paramount 3200	C53F	1983	Ex Green, Kirkintilloch, 1991
C488DKN	Renault-Dodge S56	Dormobile	C26F	1985	Ex Lytham, St Columb, 1987
E899YKO	Renault-Dodge S56	Dormobile	DP24F	1988	
E900YKO	Renault-Dodge S56	Dormobile	DP24F	1988	
H851NOC	Dennis Dart 9.8SDL3003	Carlyle Dartline	B43F	1991	

Previous Registrations:
YKN825S   WKE68S, 4066KO

TILLINGBOURNE Fleet List

Reg	Chassis	Body	Seating	Year	History
ODV404W	AEC Reliance 6U3ZR	Duple Dominant II Exp	B53F	1980	Ex Metrobus, 1991
508AHU	Volvo B10M-56	Plaxton Supreme V Exp	C53F	1982	Ex James & Williams, Treorchy, 1989
JTF971W	Leyland National 2 NL116AL11/1R		B52F	1981	Ex Kent Coach Tours, 1992
FGD827X	Volvo B10M-56	Duple Dominant	B51F	1982	Ex Graham, Paisley, 1990
FOD942Y	Dennis Dorchester SDA802	Wadham Stringer Vanguard	B59F	1983	
FOD943Y	Dennis Dorchester SDA802	Wadham Stringer Vanguard	B59F	1983	
A889FPM	Bedford YMT	Plaxton Bustler	B55F	1984	
A339HNR	Volvo B10M-56	Plaxton Paramount 3200 E	C53F	1984	Ex Woodstones, Kidderminster, 1988
B877OLJ	Leyland Tiger TRCTL11/2R	Duple Dominant	B55F	1984	
TBC658	Volvo B10M-61	Plaxton Paramount 3500	C53F	1984	Ex Ford, Gunnislake, 1990
B327KPD	Bedford YMT	Plaxton Bustler	B53F	1984	
B918NPC	Bedford YMP	Lex Maxeta	B35F	1985	Ex The Bee Line, 1988
B919NPC	Bedford YMP	Lex Maxeta	B35F	1985	Ex Alder Valley South, 1987
C195WJT	Leyland Tiger TRBTL11/2R	Duple Dominant	B53F	1985	
D424XPJ	Iveco Daily 49.10	Robin Hood	B21F	1986	
D425XPJ	Iveco Daily 49.10	Robin Hood	B21F	1986	
D694WAU	Bedford YMT	Plaxton Derwent	B60F	1987	Ex Felix, Stanley, 1988
E364NEG	Volvo B10M-61	Northern Counties Paladin(1992)	B53F	1987	Ex Cambridge CS, 1992
E215MFX	Bedford YMT	Plaxton Derwent	B53F	1987	
E216MFX	Bedford YMT	Plaxton Derwent	B53F	1987	
F870TLJ	Leyland Tiger TRBTL11/2RP	Plaxton Derwent	B52F	1988	
F914TBP	Mercedes-Benz 709D	Robin Hood	B26F	1989	Ex Tenby Bus & Coach, 1991
G401DPD	Scania K93CRB	Plaxton Derwent	B57F	1989	
	Iveco Daily 49.10	Carlyle Dailybus II	B25F	1989	

G402DPD	G403DPD	G404DPD	G405DPD	G406DPD

Reg	Chassis	Body	Seating	Year	History
G256NCL	Mercedes-Benz 814D	Reeve Burgess Beaver	C33F	1990	Ex 545 Club, Brighton, 1992
G810DPH	Iveco Daily 49.10	Phoenix	B25F	1990	
H421GPM	Mercedes-Benz 709D	Dormobile Routemaker	B27F	1990	
H422GPM	Mercedes-Benz 709D	Phoenix	B27F	1990	
H423GPM	Mercedes-Benz 709D	Phoenix	B27F	1990	
H426KPA	Mercedes-Benz 709D	Dormobile Routemaker	B27F	1990	
H427KPA	Mercedes-Benz 709D	Dormobile Routemaker	B27F	1990	
H428KPD	Mercedes-Benz 811D	Whittaker-Europa	B28F	1991	
H429KPD	Mercedes-Benz 811D	Whittaker-Europa	B28F	1991	
H11TBC	Volvo B10M-60	Ikarus Blue Danube	C53F	1991	
J430PPF	Mercedes-Benz 709D	Dormobile Routemaker	B29F	1991	
J431PPF	Iveco Daily 49.10	Carlisle Dailybus 2	B29F	1991	

Previous Registrations:
508AHU   NUH262X   TBC658   A298XUK, 353TPF, A489YGL.
LHO992Y   AEF992Y, TBC658

Named vehicles:
B918NPC *Lord Hayman of Reigate*, D424XPJ *Will*, D425XPJ *Rose*, G401DPD *The Lord Billy B*, G402DPD *Sam*, G403DPD *Pippin*, G404DPD *Frodo*, G405DPD, *Bilbo*, G406DPD *Merry*, G810DPH *Fredegar*.

Special Liveries:
Overall Advertisements: B327KPD

TOWN & AROUND Fleet List

KBU892P	Leyland National 10351/1R		B41F	1975	Ex Seabrook, Hythe, 1991
MGR528P	Leyland National 11351/1R		B49F	1975	Ex Amberley, Pudsey, 1989
UPB330S	Leyland National 10351A/1R		B41F	1977	Ex London Country SW, 1990
JSS202V	Ford R1014	Alexander AYS	B45F	1980	Ex Northern Scottish, 1988
JSS203V	Ford R1014	Alexander AYS	B45F	1980	Ex Northern Scottish, 1988
H264GKK	Leyland Swift LBM6T/2RA	Wadham Stringer Vanguard II	B39F	1991	

WARREN Fleet List

GKL825N	Bristol VRT/SL2/6LX	Eastern Coach Works	H43/34F	1974	Ex Maidstone & District, 1990
GKL827N	Bristol VRT/SL2/6LX	Eastern Coach Works	H43/34F	1974	Ex Maidstone & District, 1990
LHC919P	Bedford YMT	Duple Dominant	C45F	1976	
NFN85R	Leyland National 11351A/1R		DP48F	1977	Ex East Kent, 1990
THX146S	Leyland National 10351A/2R		B36D	1978	Ex London Buses, 1990
XAK459T	Leyland National 11351A/1R		B52F	1978	Ex Jeal, Crawley, 1990
UBK606	Leyland Leopard PSU5C/4R	Plaxton Supreme IV	C53F	1979	Ex Haynes, Christchurch, 1989
LUA274V	Leyland Leopard PSU3F/4R	Plaxton Supreme IV	C53F	1980	Ex Denslow, Chard, 1987
SPN670X	Leyland Leopard PSU3F/5R	Plaxton Supreme V	C53F	1982	Ex Worthing Coaches, 1986
B873FWA	Volvo B10M-61	Plaxton Paramount 3500 II	C53F	1985	Ex Clarke, London SE20, 1990
F829GKO	Scania K93CRB	Duple 320	C55F	1989	
TSU612	Kässbohrer Setra S210H	Kässbohrer Tornado	C28FT	1988	Ex Tours Exclusive, London W14, 1991

Previous Registrations:
UBK606   DJU59T

WEALDEN BEELINE Fleet List

HEF379N	Leyland Leopard PSU3C/4R	Plaxton Elite III Exp	DP53F	1975	Ex Danks, Oldfield, 1991
KUT587P	Leyland Leopard PSU3C/4R	Duple Dominant	B65F	1975	Ex Midland Fox, 1989
OJD235R	Leyland Fleetline FE30AGR	Park Royal	H44/28D	1977	Ex Pardes House School, 1991
976NE	Leyland Leopard PSU3C/4R	Plaxton Supreme III Exp	C53F	1976	Ex Rotherham Travel, 1990
XFA967S	Leyland Leopard PSU3C/4R	Marshall Camair	DP53F	1978	Ex Jowitt, Tankersley, 1990
TPD28S	AEC Reliance 6U2R	Duple Dominant II Express	C53F	1977	Ex Lambkin, Sheerness, 1992
ULS320T	Leyland Leopard PSU3E/4R	Alexander AYS	B53F	1979	Ex Graham, Paisley, 1990
ULS654T	Leyland Leopard PSU3E/4R	Duple Dominant	C53F	1979	Ex Kirk, Pulborough, 1992
C551NWV	Mercedes-Benz L608D	Reeve Burgess	C19F	1985	Ex Maidstone & District, 1990
G468VYE	CVE Omni	CVE	B21F	1990	Ex Fuggles, Benenden, 1992
J944MKJ	OBC Omni	OBC	DP21F	1991	
J255MKR	OBC Omni	OBC	DP20F	1991	
J459JOW	Dennis Dart 9SDL3011	Wadham Stringer Portsdown	B37F	1992	Ex Wadham Stringer demonstrator, 1992

Previous Registration:
976NE   NEL115P

WEST SUSSEX Fleet List

AP01	603BFJ	Ford R1114	Plaxton Supreme	C53F	1983	Ex Weller, Midhurst, 1989
AP02	XUX666T	Ford R1114	Plaxton Supreme IV	C53F	1978	Ex Pearce, Darch & Wilcox, 1990
AP03	KWJ865W	Ford R1114	Plaxton Supreme IV	C53F	1981	Ex Bowker, Knypersley, 1990
AP04	JMJ150V	Ford R1114	Plaxton Supreme IV	C53F	1979	Ex Elite, Stockport, 1990
AP05	JMJ110V	Ford R1114	Plaxton Supreme IV	C53F	1979	Ex Elite, Stockport, 1990
AP52	CRV849W	Ford R1014	Wadham Stringer Vanguard	B55F	1981	
AP53	CRV850W	Ford R1014	Wadham Stringer Vanguard	B55F	1981	
AP54	FTP848X	Ford R1014	Wright	B53F	1981	

AP55	FTP847X	Ford R1014	Wright	B53F	1981	
AP61	LOR772Y	Ford R1015	Wadham Stringer Vanguard	B55F	1983	
AP62	LOR773Y	Ford R1015	Wadham Stringer Vanguard	B55F	1983	
AP63	A486PPX	Ford R1015	Locomotors	B55F	1984	
AP64	A487PPX	Ford R1015	Locomotors	B55F	1984	
AR01	WNN56S	Leyland Leopard PSU5B/4R	Plaxton Supreme III	C57F	1978	Ex Skill, Nottingham, 1985
AR04	XDG213S	Leyland Leopard PSU5C/4R	Plaxton Supreme III	C57F	1978	Ex Middleton, Rugeley, 1986
AR05	CGF313S	Leyland Leopard PSU5C/4R	Plaxton Supreme III	C55F	1978	Ex Richmond, Epsom, 1987
AR06	YBN629V	Leyland Leopard PSU3E/4R	Plaxton Supreme IV	C53F	1979	Ex Howle, Smethwick, 1990
AR70	YCH890M	Bristol RELH6L	Eastern Coach Works	C49F	1974	Ex Trent, 1988
AR71	YCH891M	Bristol RELH6L	Eastern Coach Works	DP49F	1974	Ex Trent, 1988
AR72	PCH268L	Bristol RELH6L	Eastern Coach Works	DP53F	1972	Ex Trent, 1988
AR75	YCH897M	Bristol RELH6L	Eastern Coach Works	C49F	1974	Ex Trent, 1988
AR77	PCH271L	Bristol RELH6L	Eastern Coach Works	C49F	1972	Ex Trent, 1989
AV08	VOR625T	Bedford VAS5	Marshall	B33F	1979	
AX01	VPT255L	Leyland Atlantean AN68/1R	Alexander AD	H45/30D	1972	Ex Portsmouth, 1987
AX20	MOD567P	Bristol VRT/SL3/6LXB	Eastern Coach Works	H43/32F	1976	Ex Southdown, 1988
AX21	RKO811M	Bristol VRT/SL2/6LX	Eastern Coach Works	H43/34F	1974	Ex Maidstone & District, 1988

Previous Registrations:
603BFJ   OMA203Y, OB1

WESTBUS Fleet List

22	NNS235V	Ford R1114	Plaxton Supreme IV	C53F	1980	Ex Swinard, Ashford, 1986
29	DPO550W	Mercedes-Benz L508D	Robin Hood	C16F	1981	Ex Swinard, Ashford, 1986
38	A260BTY	Leyland Royal Tiger B50	Roe Doyen	C51F	1984	Ex ADP Travel, Hounslow, 1987
40	D228HMT	Van Hool TD824	Van Hool Astromega	CH55/16DT	1987	
41	D101BNV	Volvo B10M-61	Jonckheere Jubilee P599	C49FT	1987	
42	D102BNV	Volvo B10M-61	Jonckheere Jubilee P599	C49FT	1987	
43	D103BNV	Volvo B10MT-53	Jonckheere Jubilee P95	CH49/12FT	1987	
44	D104BNV	Volvo B10MT-53	Jonckheere Jubilee P95	CH49/12FT	1987	
45	D105BNV	Volvo B10MT-53	Jonckheere Jubilee P95	CH49/12FT	1987	

46-53		Volvo B10M-61	Duple 340	C53F*	1988	*46-8 are C49FT

46	E168OMU	48	E170OMU	50	E172OMU	52	E174OMU	53	E175OMU
47	E169OMU	49	E171OMU	51	E173OMU				

59	F994UME	Volvo B10M-60	Duple 340	C53F	1989
60	F995UME	Volvo B10M-60	Duple 340	C53F	1989
61	F996UME	Volvo B10M-60	Duple 340	C53F	1989

	KDW332P	Leyland National 11351/1R		B49F	1975	Ex National Welsh, 1989
	KDW339P	Leyland National 11351/1R		B49F	1975	Ex National Welsh, 1989
	KJD542P	Leyland National 10351/2R		B36D	1976	Ex London Buses, 1990
	YYE282T	Leyland National 10351A/2R		B36D	1978	Ex Fountain, Feltham, 1990
	RFS585V	Leyland National 2 NL116L11/1R		B52F	1980	Ex Sheffield United, 1990
	RFS586V	Leyland National 2 NL116L11/1R		B52F	1980	Ex Sheffield United, 1991
	RFS588V	Leyland National 2 NL116L11/1R		B52F	1980	Ex Sheffield United, 1990
	F906YNV	Volvo B10M-60	Jonckheere Deauville	C49FT	1989	
	F608WBV	Leyland Lynx LX112L10ZR1S	Leyland	B52F	1988	Ex Volvo demonstrator, 1990
	G936VRY	Leyland Lynx LX112L10ZR1R	Leyland	B51F	1990	
	H176EJF	Toyota HDB30R	Caetano Optimo	C18F	1991	
	J724KBC	Leyland Lynx LX2R11V18Z4S	Leyland	B51F	1992	

Acknowledgements:
We are grateful to David Donati, Keith Grimes, Mark Jameson, Richard Lewis, Colin Lloyd, Geoff Mills,
The M&D and East Kent Bus Club, the PSV Circle, the Southdown Enthusiasts' Club and the operating
companies for their assistance in the compilation of this book.

Contents correct to September 1992
Series Editor: Bill Potter